WORLD POWER OR DECLINE

The Controversy Over
*Germany's Aims
in the First World War*

Also by Fritz Fischer

Germany's Aims in the First World War
War of Illusions

WORLD POWER
OR DECLINE

The Controversy Over
Germany's Aims
in the First World War

FRITZ FISCHER

Translated by Lancelot L. Farrar,
Robert Kimber, and Rita Kimber

 W · W · NORTON & CO · INC · NEW YORK

Translation copyright © 1974 by W. W. Norton & Company, Inc.
Published in Germany under the title *Weltmacht oder Niedergang*
Copyright © 1965 by Europäische Verlagsanstalt, Frankfurt am Main.

Library of Congress Cataloging in Publication Data

Fischer, Fritz, 1908–
  World power or decline.

  Translation of Weltmacht oder Niedergang.
  Includes bibliographical references.
    1. European War, 1914–1918—Germany. 2. European
War, 1914–1918—Historiography. I. Title
D515.F27513   940.3'24'43   73-18318
ISBN 0-393-05451-3
ISBN 0-393-09413-8 (pbk.)

This book was designed by Paula Wiener.
The types are Melior and Times Roman.
The book was manufactured by Vail-Ballou Press, Inc.

Printed in the United States of America
1 2 3 4 5 6 7 8 9 0

Contents

Author's Foreword

The first edition of my book *Griff nach der Weltmacht* [1] appeared at the end of 1961. This study of Germany's aims in the First World War caused a considerable stir in the German press, and German historians, who have always been politically conservative as a profession, launched a bitter attack on the book. What prompted this reaction? I had apparently violated a national taboo.

Ever since the collapse of the Third Reich, historians have tended to neglect the First World War, focusing attention instead on Adolf Hitler and the Second World War. This preoccupation with the Nazi period was primarily motivated, either consciously or unconsciously, by a desire to isolate the catastrophe of Nazism from the rest of German history and to regard the Hitler phenomenon as an "aberration" or as an inexplicable curse visited on the German people.

German history before and after Hitler seemed to be "unproblematic." Such a view was possible only because German historians had provided a basis for it both during and after the First World War. They claimed that Germany's envious neighbors—France, England, and Russia—had been attempting to "hem in" the prosperous and ambitious German Reich since the turn of the century.

---

1. Published by Droste Verlag, Düsseldorf. The most recent German edition, the fourth, appeared in 1970. An abridged German edition was published in 1967, and translations have appeared in France, Italy, Japan, England, and the United States. W. W. Norton & Company, Inc., published the American edition in 1967 under the title *Germany's Aims in the First World War*.

Finally, in 1914, these Entente powers attacked, forcing Germany to defend herself. Thus, if Germany had any war aims at all, they were of a purely defensive nature.

If this was an accurate picture of Germany's role in World War I—and German schoolbooks proclaimed that it was—then there was clearly a vast difference between the two wars. In July 1914, Germany had been drawn into war; and for the next four years, she fought desperately for her very existence. In September 1939, on the other hand, Hitler deliberately precipitated war, a fact that no one in Germany will dispute; and for the next six years, he continued to pursue his grandiose plans for conquest.

For historians schooled in this tradition, my book was nothing short of treason. I had demonstrated beyond any doubt that Germany had similar aims in both world wars, and since this similarity could not be denied, my critics resorted to a variety of methods to obscure the unpleasant truth. One faction distorted my conclusions. Michael Freund accused me of portraying Bethmann Hollweg as the Hitler of 1914, and Golo Mann claimed I had transformed Bethmann Hollweg into a "monster" bent on unlimited conquests. (It should be noted that my book deals not only with the similarities but also with the differences that German war aims show in the two world wars. Genocide and the enslavement of entire nations were the exclusive domain of Nazi Germany and cannot be ascribed to Germany in World War I, despite a policy of expansion to the east.) Other critics reproached me with a "fetish for documentation." Unable to contradict the sources I had gathered, they took refuge in psychologizing. Some historians who had been highly critical, indeed, even contemptuous, of Bethmann Hollweg before 1945 now did a complete turnabout and re-evaluated the chancellor, presenting him as a good, moderate German statesman and contrasting him with the evil, immoderate General

Ludendorff. Among the proponents of this view were Hans Herzfeld and Gerhard Ritter. Ritter also led the attack on my interpretation of the July crisis, reiterating the traditional apologia for Germany and denying the very existence of German war aims in the years 1914 to 1918. According to Ritter, Germany had desired "nothing more" [sic] than equal status with Great Britain.

The German Historical Convention of 1964, held in Berlin, marked the high point of the controversy. Gerhard Ritter stated his position again, seconded by Egmont Zechlin and Erwin Hölzle. My former colleagues Imanuel Geiss and Helmut Böhme joined me in exploring domestic and social implications of German imperialism.[2] Our studies grew out of questions that had come up in the course of my work on *Griff nach der Weltmacht.* The seven theses I presented at the Convention incorporated the essential points of *Griff nach der Weltmacht,* and were subsequently published as *Weltmacht oder Niedergang (World Power or Decline),* the first volume in the series Hamburg Studies in Modern History. I am delighted to see this volume available in an American edition now, because my method and basic approach emerge more clearly in this short work than they do in my extensive study of German war aims.

The debate begun in Berlin continued at the twelfth International Historical Congress, held in Vienna in 1965. Ritter presented a paper that, for polemic and bias, surpassed all his previous efforts. Once again he limited himself to the biographical details of Bethmann Hollweg's chancellorship. According to Ritter, Bethmann Hollweg's intentions were highly ethical: the chancellor hoped to fight a "war of attrition" that would lead to a "com-

---

2. I. Geiss spoke on the July crisis of 1914. He has edited two volumes that contain all the essential documents from the powers involved in the crisis. H. Böhme spoke on the treaty of Brest Litovsk, showing how it realized the aims of German economic imperialism.

promise peace." The evidence is to the contrary. German policy called for a blitzkrieg and rapid victory. In my paper,[3] which drew on both east and west European sources, I tried to show what the political, social, economic, religious, and intellectual forces were that had produced this policy.

The meeting in Vienna by no means put an end to the controversy. Discussion of the questions *Griff nach der Weltmacht* had raised continued for years, not only in academic circles but also on the radio, on television, and in the press. A great number of studies on the First World War, many of which have since appeared in book form, resulted from this discussion. The "Fischer controversy," now history itself, has been analyzed in numerous publications. In 1966, the fifth number of the *Journal of Contemporary History* printed a collection of essays that reviewed the controversy up to that time. This collection appeared a year later in Germany under the title *Kriegsausbruch 1914*. A still more thorough presentation of the controversy can be found in John A. Moses' essay, "The War Aims of Imperial Germany: Professor Fritz Fischer and His Critics." [4] In this study, the author undertakes a detailed analysis of my critics.

Since the "Fischer controversy" had revolved primarily around the first two chapters of *Griff nach der Weltmacht*, my next major book, published in 1969, dealt with the questions those chapters had raised. This later study, *Krieg der Illusionen* (*War of Illusions*), covers the period from the Agadir crisis to the outbreak of war, examining not only military and diplomatic factors but also the economic, social, and domestic forces affecting German war aims. I was able to prove that German policy during

3. The paper I delivered at the Congress was published in *Actes du Comité International des Sciences Historiques* (Vienna, 1967), pp. 721 ff.
4. *University of Queensland Papers, Department of Government and History*, I, No. 4 (1967), 214–260.

World War I did in fact have its origins in the prewar
period and that Germany's war aims on the continent,
both in the east and in the west, took shape as the German
effort to acquire an overseas empire suffered one setback
after another in 1905, 1908, 1911, and 1912–13. I was
also able to prove that war with France and Russia was
considered "inevitable" and that the decision to embark
on this war—if possible with an assurance of English
neutrality for at least the initial phases of the conflict—
dated from December 1912, if not earlier. This book gave
rise to fresh controversy both in the press and in academic
circles, but the debate was not as violent and bitter as it
had been in the past because the central theses of *Griff
nach der Weltmacht* had already been assimilated into
German historiography and had even made their way
into reference books and school texts. I am very pleased
that *Krieg der Illusionen,* too, will appear in both England and America, published by Chatto & Windus in
London and by W. W. Norton & Company in New
York. Alan Bullock, author of the most important study
of Hitler to date, will write the preface for the English
and American editions.

In his foreword to the American edition of *Griff nach
der Weltmacht,* Hajo Holborn emphasized the continuity
in German policy from the First World War to the Second, noting at the same time the crucial differences between the wars. He also called attention to the profound
change that the awareness of this undeniable continuity
has brought about in historical thinking everywhere, but
particularly in Germany itself. Jacques Droz wrote in
his preface to the French edition of *Griff nach der Weltmacht* that the book represents a "milestone" in German
history. Droz goes on to say that *Griff nach der Weltmacht*
had obviously stirred the political conscience of Germany and destroyed many a treasured illusion. He points
out that Bethmann Hollweg was by no means a precursor

of Hitler and that I never portrayed him as such. But Droz does make clear that Hitler could not have come to power so easily if German historians had not deceived the public, both during and after World War I, about Germany's aims in that war and if they had not lent support to the power politics and expansionist aspirations of Wilhelminian imperialism.

Whether *Griff nach der Weltmacht* and *Krieg der Illusionen* have indeed worked such a catharsis in the historical and political consciousness of Germany is a question that foreign observers and later generations will better be able to judge than I. But it cannot be denied that a profound change has taken place in the thinking of German historians and of the public at large, a change that should help Germany arrive at a more realistic self-appraisal than she has been willing to undertake in the past. More important still, it should also make her more willing to accept the consequences of the Second World War.

FRITZ FISCHER

Introduction

The omnipresence of cold war issues caused many historians to concentrate their attention immediately after 1945 on the Second World War. But in recent years the Second World War has been seen increasingly as part of a larger phenomenon variously characterized as the second Thirty Years' War, the European civil war, the end of European history, and the beginning of world history. It is a phenomenon that began with the outbreak of the First World War, and many of its critical events—the dissolution of the Russian, Habsburg, German, and Ottoman Empires and the emergence of the United States as a world power—occurred during the war itself. Deeper and more subtle changes followed from the first total and global conflict. Government control over opinion, ideology, the press, the economy, and society not only provided the model for totalitarian experiments, but also left its mark on democratic societies. The First World War can thus be said to be the beginning of a new ideological era of which the cold war is only one chapter. By its expansion into a global conflict and its simultaneous weakening of the European powers, the war altered the relationship between the developed, imperialist societies of the North Atlantic and the less developed areas of the world, especially those under colonial rule. Although it ended with the extension of European colonialism, the seeds of the colonial demise had been sown and would be reaped after the Second World War. In short, many of the problems of the second half of the twentieth century have grown out of a process which began in 1914.

Although there has been general agreement on the importance of the First World War, there has been little on its meaning. As with most major historical events, historians, politicians, and laymen have seen in it what they chose to see. Immediately after the war, many historians focused on the question of its origins because of the assertion in the Versailles Treaty that Germany had been responsible for the war. During the 1920s, the participants in this debate usually asserted that one state or side was guilty and the other innocent, but by the 1930s many had come to Lloyd George's conclusion that the war had been due less to evil intent than to stupidity: "The nations slithered over the brink into the boiling cauldron of war without any trace of apprehension or dismay." [1]

Other historians concentrated on the military events— the winners seeking to explain why they had won or why they had not won sooner, the losers to explain why they had not or why they should have. In both cases, the war was regarded as a lesson for future wars—for some what not to do, for others what to do better.

Some—most notably but not exclusively Hitler— drew from the war morals which could be applied to the social and economic aspects of another war. Some drew the opposite conclusion: precisely the totality of the First World War made it inconceivable that Europe would fight another. After another total war had ended in 1945, the perception of the First World War changed again. The immediacy, scope, and horror of World War II partially obscured the impact of World War I. There was, however, a difference between the reaction of Germans and that of other peoples to this experience. Non-Germans —particularly those who had already been convinced

---

1. David Lloyd George, *War Memoirs* (London, 1938), vol. I, p. 32.

of German responsibility for World War I—generally regarded World War II as confirmation of their conclusion. In contrast, many, perhaps most, Germans tended to see Nazism and World War II as an aberration and departure from previous German history. These Germans therefore tended to look back on the First World War with clear consciences, even perhaps some pride, and considerable nostalgia.

The perception of World War I and Germany's role in it was altered radically during the 1960s. This revision was precipitated by the work of Professor Fritz Fischer of the University of Hamburg. As one historian commented recently, the 1960s were "Fritz Fischer's decade." In between the publication of his two major books in 1961 and 1969, "there has been more discussion, scholarly and otherwise, than has been caused by any other single historian in our lifetime." [2] The extent of this discussion has been impressive indeed—literally scores of reviews, responses and counter-responses, conferences and debates, radio programs, and full-length books.[3] Perhaps even more notable and historically significant have been the non-academic side-effects. The debate caused a reaction in Germany which was sufficiently emotional as to be described as consternation. After publishing extracts from Fischer's first book, the *Time*-like magazine *Der Spiegel* was bombarded for weeks with vitriolic letters to the editor. The mood of many older Germans may have been summed up in the remark of one of Fischer's colleagues at the University of Hamburg: "He has destroyed my *Weltanschauung!*" The discussion apparently reflected a generation gap, with most older Germans opposing

2. Joachim Remak, "1914—The Third Balkan War: Origins Reconsidered," *Journal of Modern History*, September 1971, p. 353.
3. For the debate over German policy, see Ernst W. Graf Lynar, *Deutsche Kriegsziele, 1914–1918* (Frankfurt am Main and Berlin, 1964), which has a long bibliography, and Wolfgang Schieder, *Erster Weltkrieg, Ursachen, Entstehung und Kriegsziele* (Cologne and Berlin), 1969.

Fischer and younger Germans supporting him. As a result of the furor, support for Fischer's planned visit to the United States was withdrawn by a German government agency. The trip was eventually funded by an American foundation after a protest by American professors, led by the historian John Snell. Clearly, Fischer had touched a sensitive nerve and demonstrated not only that the writing of history itself can become a historical phenomenon but also that the self-image of a society can be deeply involved with its own past.

What had Fischer written that could justify such a response? After a decade of research into the official German documents, Fischer produced a massive work entitled *Griff nach der Weltmacht*.[4] He argued that the First World War had "become history and can be made the object of dispassionate consideration. This book is therefore neither an indictment nor a defense." Thus, it was not the historian's role "to accuse or defend." Despite this disclaimer, Fischer's book had the effect of an indictment of German behavior before and during the First World War. He concluded that "consciousness of strength, an urge for expansion and a need for security combined to mold the policy of Wilhelm II's Germany." These elements caused "certain mental attitudes and aspirations which were active in German policy during the First World War and remained operative later." In this sense, he felt his study might "serve as a contribution toward the problem of the continuity of German policy from the First World War to the Second." The object of this policy during the First World War was "to weld continental 'Mitteleuropa' into a force which would place Germany on equal terms with the established and potential world

4. *Griff nach der Weltmacht, Die Kriegszielpolitik des kaiserlichen Deutschland, 1914–1918* (Düsseldorf, 1961), translated as *Germany's Aims in the First World War*, published in 1967 by W. W. Norton & Company in the United States and Chatto & Windus Ltd. in Great Britain.

powers: the British Empire, Russia, and the United States." [5] As the German title of the book expressed succinctly, Germany had made a "grab for world power" status during the First World War.

Fischer's views were attacked on methodological and substantive grounds. His critics argued that his method was not the detached account of events which he had claimed, but rather a prejudiced and purposeful indictment of German policy apparently motivated by the experience of World War II. They therefore rejected his thesis of continuity between German behavior before, during, and after the two world wars, and reiterated the interpretation that both wars had constituted sharp breaks in German history. Similarly, they defended German conduct against Fischer's charge that Germany bore primary responsibility for the outbreak of war in 1914. Some revived the argument that other states had been primarily responsible, some that all had been partially responsible, and some that the war had been a mistake. Fischer's critics also refused to accept his view of German war aims, and asserted that Germany had pursued expansionist objectives only inconsistently, unconsciously, and in response to wartime pressures; in any case, German behavior was no worse than that of other powers in the "age of imperialism." They doubted Fischer's contention that most Germans had favored the stated war aims, renewing the claim that only a few extremists had desired expansion and imposed their will on the moderate majority. In short, they voiced the traditional view of German history.

Fischer defended his position tenaciously in the press, at conferences, and above all in this book and in a larger study published in 1969 entitled *Krieg der Illusionen*.[6]

5. Quoted from the American edition, pp. xxi–xxii.
6. *Krieg der Illusionen, Die deutsche Politik von 1911 bis 1914* (Düsseldorf, 1969).

In the present book, he concentrates on the wartime period after a cursory discussion of prewar questions. In *Krieg der Illusionen* he focused on the prewar period, arguing more extensively than he had done previously that German policy was basically the same before and after the outbreak of war in 1914.

The present book, *World Power or Decline,* published in 1965 under the title of *Weltmacht oder Niedergang,*[7] provides perhaps the best summary of Fischer's general conception and the issues, as he sees them, in the heated debate. Like other disputes—particularly over emotional questions—this one tended to polarize the issues in a way which the participants seem neither to have intended nor anticipated. While this polarization probably exaggerates disagreements, it nonetheless points up some very real differences in assumptions and conclusions not only about German history but also about the nature and function of history in general.

Characteristically, Fischer gave the book a provocative title—*World Power or Decline*—a phrase that appeared in the extreme nationalist writings of the Prussian General Friedrich Bernhardi, who had urged Germany to prepare for the coming war. Fischer seeks to meet his critics on the substantive and methodological levels. In Part I, on factual criticism, he isolates what he calls his seven "theses." In the first of these, he summarizes his argument (set forth in greater detail in *Krieg der Illusionen*) that the outbreak of war in 1914 caused no discontinuity in German policy; German wartime aims were merely the logical extension and codification of prewar aspirations for world power. His second thesis is that, far from opposing war in July 1914, the German government consciously provoked it because of domestic and diplomatic considerations. In response to his critics' assertion that German war aims were only occasionally and temporarily

7. *Weltmacht oder Niedergang, Deutschland im ersten Weltkrieg* (Hamburg, 1965).

extensive as a result of momentary military success, he argues in his third thesis that the ambitious war aims program of September 1914 remained the blueprint for German policy throughout the war. In his fourth and fifth theses, he claims that German policy during the war is best understood not as a response to a series of crises and wartime problems but rather as a consistent and active commitment to expansion. His sixth point is the contention that these aspirations were not limited to a few extremists or even to the government in general but were shared by the mass of Germans. Finally, he argues in his seventh thesis that military victory was seen by most members of the German ruling class as a means for preserving the conservative political system.

In Part II, on methodological questions, Fischer typically seeks not only to parry the attacks but also to launch counterattacks. He first takes on Egmont Zechlin, a colleague on the history faculty of the University of Hamburg and a generation older than Fischer. With some modifications, Zechlin had revived the conventional argument that Germany had behaved as a typical imperialist power. In Zechlin's view, the German government was motivated during July 1914 primarily by anxiety over the possibility that Britain would join France and Russia to encircle Germany and lure away Germany's primary ally, Austria-Hungary. Zechlin then applied this reactive interpretation to German wartime policy, maintaining that it was makeshift and pragmatic rather than rigid and consistent. Fischer quite correctly contends that the dispute with Zechlin reflects differing methods and assumptions. Each draws on virtually the same materials to buttress his view: Fischer chooses those facts which emphasize consistency, Zechlin those which demonstrate contradictions.

Fischer's other primary antagonist was the late Gerhard Ritter, the generally acknowledged dean of German historians, professor at the University of Freiburg, and also a generation older than Fischer. Like Zechlin, Ritter defended many of the previously accepted interpretations of German history. Far from seeking world power, Germany had been forced into the conflict against her will and had fought essentially a defensive war. Only when control of German policy was usurped by the extremists during the war had German policy perhaps warranted the criticism Fischer leveled at it. Ritter therefore distinguishes among situations and statesmen, whereas Fischer sees more continuity and conformity. Thus, a fundamentally different method is applied: Ritter chooses to emphasize the differences, Fischer the similarities. Each criticizes the other's method as misrepresentative and tendentious because it is based on preconceived assumptions. Each believes that social issues are at stake in the debate. Ritter is concerned lest what he regards as excessive emphasis on the negative aspects of German history should have damaging effects on Germany in the future, whereas Fischer implies that facing the past will be therapeutic. Likewise, each attributes motives to the other: Ritter sees Fischer's views as a reflection of guilt feelings about the Second World War, whereas Fischer attributes Ritter's to personal experiences in the First World War. In short, each finds the other's historical method preconditioned by personal factors.

Implied in the debate between Fischer and his critics are large questions about European history and international relations. Is the European experience in the twentieth century better conceived as a continuum or as distinct periods caused by a series of crises? How is foreign policy conceived? How are ends affected by means? How do circumstances alter aims? These questions bear on the individual statesman's role in how much he is affected by current ideas and preconceptions, by the social and administrative structure, by the political and economic "realities" of the situation. In short, how much choice and thus responsibility can he realistically be said to have?

The debate involves the general question of how wars

begin—because of design, mistake, or circumstances beyond the control of statesmen or even the comprehension of historians? Another central but complex question involves the relationship between government, interest groups, the military, the political parties, and the people, that is, between foreign policy and public opinion. Behind much of the discussion is the ultimate question of international politics, namely, power: Was it possible for a state like Germany to pursue any but an aggressive policy when its power was inordinately large relative to the other members of the state system?

Finally, the debate is adequate testimony that history can arouse considerable emotion. While the dispute over method demonstrates that history is a far more creative process than merely placing facts in chronological order, it also reveals the importance of basic assumptions that may in fact have been conditioned by the experience of the individual historian and his generation. These assumptions underlie not only the historian's interpretation but also his very conception of the purpose of written history.

Like good history in general, this book raises questions to which there are no final answers. Ideally, it will encourage the reader to pursue these issues in the larger works of Fischer and the other participants in the debate. Although many of the works cited in the debate are not available in translation, the major works of both Fischer and Ritter either have been or will soon be published in English.[8]

Seattle, Washington　　　　　LANCELOT L. FARRAR
November 1972

8. The English translation of Fischer's *Krieg der Illusionen* is to be published in 1973 by Chatto & Windus Ltd. in Great Britain and W. W. Norton & Company in the United States, under the title *War of Illusions*. Ritter's three-volume *Staatskunst und Kriegshandwerk, Das Problem des "Militarismus" in Deutschland* is being translated and will be published by the University of Miami Press under the title of *The Sword and the Scepter*.

A Note on Translation

A few words should be said about the translation. All translators must confront the choice between content and style. Although Professor Fischer is more concerned with his argument than with literary form, he does have a particular style which is pithy, alliterative, assertive, and provocative—in short, appropriate to a debate of this kind. We have sought to convey this style as much as possible. A first draft of the translation was prepared by Lancelot L. Farrar and the final translation by Robert and Rita Kimber.

Since *World Power or Decline* draws on considerable source material already used in the German edition of *Germany's Aims in the First World War* (*Griff nach der Weltmacht*), the footnotes in this book use the same abbreviations that were employed in the documentation of *Griff nach der Weltmacht*. We have written out only the name of the archives in which a certain document can be found, e.g., Deutsches Zentralarchiv, Potsdam = DZA Potsdam. The subheadings are left in abbreviated form, and the interested reader is referred to the list of abbreviations in *Griff nach der Weltmacht* as well as to the extensive bibliography contained in that volume.

WORLD POWER
OR DECLINE

The Controversy Over
Germany's Aims
in the First World War

PART ONE

In Response to Factual Criticism

> The question is one of victory or extinction, not one of gain or loss in power or territory. If we win—and anyone who doubts we shall is a cur—we can impose our rules on the conquered world and give things the shape necessary for our own development and for the good of the small neighboring peoples that flock around us and look to us for protection and salvation.
>
> Johannes Haller, in
> *Süddeutsche Monatshefte,*
> September 1914

World Policy and War Policy: Germany's Persisting Desire for World Power

German historical writing has traditionally seen the First World War and the "Age of Imperialism" as separate entities. In this view, new factors determined the policies of all the countries involved in the war. I would argue, to the contrary, that it is untenable to separate national policies during the war from those before it. That holds true for all the major powers. Imperialistic impulses, hunger for prestige, and expansionist desires characterize them all. But in sharp contrast to England, France, Russia, and the United States, Germany alone considered her place among the major powers incommensurate with her potential as the most industrialized country on the continent. She had sixty-eight million inhabitants and a yearly increase of over 850,000 people; she had a cultural tradition and a political system distinct from those of western democracy and of eastern despotism. Under Bismarck, Germany had attained an equal position among the European powers, but now she set out consciously and with determination to become a "world power."[1] However, within a single decade (1897–1907) the expansionist impulse of German politics and of the German economy had led to an isolation that Germany had brought upon herself but that she interpreted as an "encirclement" or an "iron ring" imposed from without.[2]

From then on, "breaking up the Entente" became Germany's most important goal. Gaining "freedom of movement" was considered the prerequisite for Germany's further development and for her steady climb to the rank of a world power. It was the feeling of "the nation" that if Germany did not gain this "freedom," she would have to relinquish her place in the world. In the thinking of the time, Germany was locked in single combat with England. As late as 1919, General Groener stressed this view in a speech before the general staff and emphasized that Germany—even if unconsciously—had "striven for world dominion" and had tried "to wrest it from England."[3] Max Weber—along with many others of the German intellectual elite—shared this opinion.[4] The highly respected General Bernhardi, ghostwriter for Germany's top military officers, formulated the same idea in his book *Deutschland und der nächste Krieg* (*Germany and the Next War*). The central and often-cited motto of the book, which had gone through six printings by 1914, was "world power or decline." Under this banner "the nation" came together, fought, and hoped to conquer. The picture of Wilhelminian Germany that Ger-

1. Let me make one thing clear from the start: Contrary to what some of my critics suggest, I do not claim that Germany was intent on world domination, even though this idea was in circulation in the prewar period.
2. Deutsches Zentralarchiv, Potsdam, Jagow Papers.
3. Bundesarchiv, Koblenz (Militärarchiv), Schleicher Papers, H 08–42/12, pp. 31–49. Speech of the Chief Quartermaster General, Supreme Headquarters, May 2, 1919.
4. M. Weber, "Nationalstaat und Volkswirtschaftspolitik" (Akademische Antrittsrede 1895), *Politische Schriften*, 2nd ed. (Tübingen, 1958), pp. 1–25.

hard Ritter and Egmont Zechlin present is a simplistic account both of the forces at work in the country and of its will to power. The methods and emphasis my critics use to depict the Germany of this time might be appropriate to a nation in the eighteenth or early nineteenth century but not to Prusso-Germany, whose structure had been changed by the industrial revolution. The government leadership and the classes supporting it were still guided by bureaucratic and agrarian notions and interests. But equally important were forces that had emerged with industrialization and capitalism. These new forces grew more insistent in their demand for recognition. This must be kept in mind in judging German imperialism. Germany's course in 1914 was determined less by her agrarian-feudal leadership than by the tension between industrial power and agrarian interests. This tension, which had already made itself felt under Bismarck, was overshadowed and offset, as it were, by still another—the tension between a patriarchical concept of life and government, based on land ownership or industrial power, and the demands of the wage-earning masses, who were developing a political consciousness.

This tension increasingly affected both the formulation of goals and the pace of activity in foreign policy, because this polarity in the evolving German situation dictated a policy of constant compromises, whether between agrarians and industrialists or between Conservatives, Liberals, and Center. The Social Democrats existed outside the orbit of all these groups, yet it was the Social Democrats with whom these groups had to deal. The origins of this dilemma go back to Bismarck and to 1879, for Bismarck's Germany was built on solidarity between the "producing classes." This solidarity, laboriously created to meet the revolutionary danger, was based on a balance of special interests: protective tariffs and tax reform for the agrarians, protective tariffs and export assistance for the industrialists, and, for the workers, an increase in the cost of living as well as a law banning the Social Democratic Party.[5] But shortly after 1879 the latent conflicts erupted again and crippled Bismarck's system: a system of accommodations in domestic policy, and, in foreign policy, a system of temporary alliances in which the tie with Austria-Hungary was the only stable factor. By 1890 Berlin was no longer completely certain of even this ally.[6] The idea of "using a preventive war to unify the nation" came up briefly in 1890 but was rejected at that time in favor of an active trade and foreign policy. Caprivi, too, failed because of the "given nature" of German politics. Indeed, the conflicts intensified during his tenure and could not be resolved until 1896–97 when the solidarity of the "producing classes" was revitalized by the new naval policy and the slogan of "world politics." These innovations allayed domestic unrest and gave the nation a unifying and convincing ideal of German greatness and power. The year 1896–97 thus marks the end of the nineteenth century for Germany. German policy broke away from the old order of the major European powers and entered into the emerging struggle for world power.

The idea of building a fleet—an idea designed to combat political stagnation at home—could be made acceptable to the major landowners, the lower-middle-class Liberals, and the Center only by creating the impression and encouraging the fear that Germany was in grave danger. This would have to be accomplished by a propaganda campaign that appealed to Germany's desire for a political role in the world commensurate with her economic and military power. As Tirpitz realized, the nation as a whole would have to accept both an image of itself as a world power and the consequent necessity of naval power before the Reichstag would approve the fleet. Germany's professors readily

5. On this problem, see H. Böhme, *Deutschlands Weg zur Grossmacht* (Cologne and Berlin, 1966).
6. H. Böhme is preparing an extensive study on this question.

accepted the patriotic duty of spreading this message.[7] In short, the idea of "encirclement" was born along with the naval policy and before there was any sign of the Entente. This argument for building a fleet had to be exploited and amplified more and more in the course of the next twelve years until it became a staple of Admiralty propaganda, and in the course of these same twelve years, the danger of "encirclement," which had at first been used as a mere pretext for expanding the navy, gradually became a bitter reality.

During the first great "fleet crisis," the Transvaal affair, the basic elements of German world policy became clear: overemphasis of economic interests, alleged national needs and security requirements, and insistence on a free hand as an equal power. This policy had the dual purpose of quelling domestic unrest and enhancing Germany's position as a major power. In the Transvaal affair, this policy led to the first serious misunderstandings with both England and Russia.

Every diplomatic defeat that Germany suffered drove her on to new ventures in the international arena, and her actions were consistently characterized by crude, high-handed power politics. The much-cited crises before the First World War illustrate this pattern. For example, diplomatic and economic considerations were not the only factors involved in the first Moroccan crisis of 1905–6. The Russian Revolution of December 1905 also had an impact on the decisions of the German government. This was particularly evident in the case of the Kaiser. It is true that Wilhelm II was "indecisive," and that, unlike Schlieffen in the General Staff and Holstein in the Foreign Ministry, he did not want to exploit the favorable situation to launch a war. But the reason for this can be found in the Kaiser's concern for the domestic as well as the international scene. It was

7. E. Zechlin, *Historische Zeitschrift,* 199, pp. 430–34.

this dual concern—German aspirations for power abroad and the desire for conservative realignment of the nation at home—that influenced his thinking during the Christmas season and found expression in the instructions he issued to his chancellor: "First shoot down, behead, and eliminate the Socialists, if necessary by a bloodbath, then go on to a foreign war. But not before, and only at the proper time." [8]

At the same time, the Kaiser ordered the diplomatic preparations for such a war. He urged alliances with Turkey, Japan, Bulgaria, and Serbia, and ordered the encouragement of insurrections in the Islamic world. In the first Morocco crisis, as was often the case, the facts bore no relation to Wilhelm's ambitions or to the government's less blatantly proclaimed aspirations. Counting on American support, Germany went to Algeciras expecting a diplomatic success, but was rebuffed in her demands. America drew back from Germany and "supported" England and France. Even the Triple Alliance showed signs of strain because Italy and Austria-Hungary by no means supported Germany without reservations. Furthermore, Algeciras turned Germany against conferences and hardened her determination to depend increasingly on the production of arms and on military strength. This rigidity characterized Germany's position at the second disarmament conference at The Hague. But domestic as well as international concerns shaped this attitude, too. Renewed arms production was also a response to the growing social danger at home.

Germany's actions in the Boer War and in the years 1898–1901, culminating in an "all or nothing" ultimatum directed at England, had brought France and England together and set the stage for their understanding with Russia. In the years 1905 and 1906, German policy led to an agreement between England and Russia that in its initial

8. B. von Bülow, *Denkwürdigkeiten,* ed. Frz. von Stockhammern, vol. II (Berlin, 1930), p. 198.

form barred Germany from certain areas overseas, such as Persia.

During this decade of "world policy," Germany had competed with the other powers in developing colonial interests. She had been active in East Asia, in South and Central America, and especially in Africa. She also showed increasing interest in the Balkans and in the Ottoman Empire, where the Baghdad railroad was the focus of her involvement.[9]

Every German venture brought with it the danger of a new loss of prestige, and each such loss called for a new show of power. A case in point is the "Bosnian crisis" of 1908, in which Germany defended Austria-Hungary's annexation of Bosnia and Herzegovina, and, by threat of arms, forced a still weakened Russia to accept it. Here, as at every possible opportunity, Germany tried to exploit a triumph over Russia to draw England (by means of the tactless *Daily Telegraph* article) and France to her side. This effort to win England and France was one of Bülow's last acts before his resignation. But this diplomatic action, too, can be completely understood only in relation to domestic political events; for at this same time, in the battle over financial reform, the agrarian-feudal, monarchical-conservative nature of Germany reasserted itself. It was not deemed necessary to win popular support for the state and to integrate the masses into the newly stabilized order, because a confrontation with Germany's eastern and western neighbors seemed more and more inevitable.

The task of keeping the Social Democrats "cooperative" was one of the goals the Kaiser set for the chancellor, Bethmann Hollweg, who took office three months after the war crisis of March 1909. Recourse to martial law remained an

9. F. Fischer, *Griff nach der Weltmacht,* 3rd ed. (Düsseldorf, 1964), pp. 15 ff; F. Fischer, "Weltpolitik, Weltmachtstreben und deutsche Kriegsziele," *Historische Zeitschrift,* 199 (1964), pp. 265 ff., 280 ff.

alternative. After 1909, and more intensively after 1912, the Prussian civil ministers and the War Ministry worked out plans for the imposition of martial law in case of a conflagration. Provisions were made for transferring domestic authority to the commanding generals and, if necessary, for the internment of the opposition leaders of the Social Democrats. These measures, combined with conscription, were felt to be adequate protection against the "revolutionary masses."

The simultaneous display of both friendship and force also characterized German policy toward England. The second task for the new chancellor was to win a "free hand" on the continent and come to terms with England. One approach was to bring England and Germany together by seeking agreement on common interests. The other was to force England into a peaceful compromise by means of pressure and threats: building a fleet, playing up the pursuit of continental alliances, and asserting German readiness for war, as during the second Moroccan crisis.

Bethmann Hollweg and his foreign secretaries, first Kiderlen-Wächter and then Jagow, adhered to these policy lines. Bethmann Hollweg, following in the tradition of his family, played a conciliatory role, while the foreign secretary assumed a strongly assertive and openly demanding one. The risk of this policy was, however, that Kiderlen-Wächter had difficulty in restraining the Pan-Germanic following he had evoked in 1911 and that Bethmann Hollweg had similar difficulty in quelling the national enthusiasm he had aroused with his speeches in 1914.

German historiography presents these two aspects of German policy toward England as fundamentally opposed. Bethmann Hollweg stands for the one, Tirpitz for the other; and they are frequently contrasted as "good" and "evil." In describing the conflict between Bethmann Hollweg and Tirpitz over policy toward England, historians have too readily forgotten that both approaches had the common goal of tying England to Germany or at least of separating England from the Entente; for after 1910 England increasingly became the main factor in German political calculations. Since 1897 Germany had pursued "world policy" and geared the "nation" toward colonial, maritime, and economic acquisitions, but without results. This policy had brought no gains in power; on the contrary, Germany's naval policy and her erratic behavior on many occasions had caused her rivals for world power to close ranks in the Entente. The reality and effectiveness of this Entente was impressed on Germany during the second Moroccan crisis. Once again the Germans came away empty-handed, but this time their parliamentarians gave them—in addition to the "traditional enemy," France—a new "arch-enemy," England. But even after the debacle of the second Moroccan crisis, Bethmann Hollweg still hoped for agreement with England. Indeed, at this point he believed both England and Germany were ready to accept such an agreement.

He hoped to greatly improve Germany's "chances for peace with England" by reducing naval appropriations in the budget of 1912, and argued that agreement with England would further German policies: "We will be able to establish a great colonial empire (Portuguese colonies, Belgian Congo, Dutch colonies) and drive a wedge into the Triple Entente (we have already succeeded in prying Russia loose from it). The Navy should certainly receive funds for personnel, U-boats, etc., but not for any more dreadnoughts." [10] Bethmann Hollweg thus returned to the alternative that Kiderlen-Wächter had already outlined during the Morocco negotiations. A German central Africa had become a clearly defined policy goal; and to reassure England, an ostensible limitation of the fleet was to be offered. In the discussions during the so-called Haldane mis-

---

10. *Der Kaiser . . . Aufzeichnungen des Chefs des Marinekabinetts Admirals Georg Alexander von Müller über die Ära Wilhelms II,* ed. W. Görlitz (Göttingen, 1964), p. 107.

sion of February 1912, this Mittelafrika plan, which called for a German "belt" all the way across Africa, appeared again as a German policy goal.[11] After failing to achieve the main political goal of the Haldane mission and after refusing to alter her naval policy, Germany persisted until the summer of 1914 in her efforts to negotiate colonial interests with England. Bethmann Hollweg and the Foreign Ministry still hoped that resort to technical agreements could weaken the Entente, resolve Anglo-German differences, and bring about an Anglo-German rapprochement.[12] The project of "consolidating Mittelafrika" (Kühlmann's phrase of autumn 1912) [13] would, in a more ambitious form, become the prime colonial goal during the war. Efforts to insure German interests in the Near East (defining the scope of the Baghdad railroad) and goals in central Africa (partition of the Portuguese colonies) also figured in the Anglo-German discussions.

Although the resulting agreement was only initialed and did not satisfy all Germany's demands in concrete terms, Bethmann Hollweg hoped he had created with it a "satisfactory basis for meeting the needs of the near future." [14] As the records of the Haldane mission show, the primary goal of German policy toward England was a guarantee of English neutrality in case of a continental war, and Bethmann Hollweg hoped he had reached some understanding with England on this point even without a binding treaty. But the chancellor could not obtain a promise of neutrality from England in the spring of 1912, nor could he induce

11. F. Fischer, *Griff nach der Weltmacht*, p. 31; F. Fischer, *Historische Zeitschrift*, 199, pp. 287–89.
12. R. von Kühlmann spoke of the "strengthening of the Triple Alliance by drawing England into the commercial activity of the Alliance." A. von Tirpitz, *Der Aufbau der deutschen Weltmacht* (Berlin, 1924), p. 389.
13. Auswärtiges Amt Bonn, Türkei 203, no. 1, vol. 2, Memorandum of Kiderlen-Wächter of October 3, 1912.
14. *Grosse Politik,* vol. XXXVII, I, no. 14709, Bethmann Hollweg to Lichnowsky, May 29, 1914, draft by W. von Stumm.

her to accept the formal alliance that had been discussed repeatedly by German leaders that year.[15] England was not prepared to guarantee neutrality in a European war. Tirpitz attempted to exert pressure on England with his new appropriation to expand the fleet. England did not yield to this pressure, but she had other reasons for refusing neutrality, too. The English government was convinced that an assurance of neutrality would give Germany a free hand to defeat France.[16] German aims in seeking a political agreement with England were, in fact, much more extensive than Bethmann Hollweg could reveal in the negotiations. Using a political alliance for mutual defense as a basis,[17] he hoped to build a central and west European political and economic system that would include France and be under German control. Influenced by Walter Rathenau (and probably by Bernhardi's recently published book), Wilhelm II developed a plan for a "United States of Europe." Rathenau and Admiral von Müller both mention this.[18] The danger American economic power posed to Europe would presumably arouse England's interest in such a plan. If the five European states—England, France, Germany, Austria-Hungary, and Italy—were joined together economically, they could hold their own against America. According to the plan the impact of an Anglo-German alliance would force France and the smaller European states to join this economic federation.

In addition to this ambitious scheme for a "United States of Europe" based on an Anglo-German alliance, Rathenau presented the chancellor and the Kaiser with a more limited

15. *Der Kaiser . . .* , ed. W. Görlitz, p. 118.
16. *British Documents*, vol. VI, no. 564, F. Bertie to E. Grey, April 3 and 6, 1912, and the minutes of E. A. Crowe and A. Nicolson.
17. *Der Kaiser . . .* , ed. W. Görlitz, p. 118.
18. Wilhelm II spoke of this to Rathenau at the home of Admiral Hollmann on February 13, 1912. For the problem of Mitteleuropa, see the dissertation of my student J. Pragal. See also: F. Fischer, *Historische Zeitschrift*, 199, p. 324; and *Der Kaiser . . .* , ed. W. Görlitz, pp. 110 ff.

Mitteleuropa plan. This plan projected a "customs union, along with closer association, to include Austria, Switzerland, Italy, Belgium, the Netherlands, etc." [19] This Mitteleuropa plan, with or without France, was to unite Germany's neighbors economically, then politically; and during the next two years it became a focal point of German policy discussions.

The acquisition of the desired central African colonies proved to be more difficult than expected, and Germany's position in the Near East and in the Balkans became more critical because she encountered the growing presence of England, France, and Russia there. In addition, the new Turkish nationalism, which had come to life after 1908 and surged up again in the summer of 1913, put off plans for partition indefinitely. The more the Entente obstructed German policy in these areas, the more significant Mitteleuropa plans became. As Rathenau said on December 25, 1913, "the opportunity for great German acquisitions has been missed. Woe to us that we took nothing and received nothing." [20] He contended that Germany, as the "most populous, strongest, richest, most industrialized country of Europe," had a rightful claim on more territory. "Since outright appropriation is out of the question, the only alternative left" was "to strive for a central European customs union that the western states would sooner or later join, like it or not. This would create an economic union that would be equal, or perhaps even superior, to America."

In addition to its anti-Americanism, this idea also had an anti-Russian bias. A unified Mitteleuropa would block any Russian policy moves directed at the Balkans or the straits and prevent any expansion of the "Slavs" into central Eu-

19. F. Fischer, *Historische Zeitschrift,* 199, p. 324.
20. W. Rathenau, "Deutsche Gefahren und neue Ziele," *Wiener Neue Freie Presse,* December 25, 1913, quoted from W. Rathenau, *Zur Kritik der Zeit, Mahnung und Warnung* (Berlin, 1925).

rope. This idea reappeared in the famous conversation between Bethmann Hollweg and the English ambassador, Goschen, in the late evening of July 29, 1914.[21] Rathenau formulated it again for Bethmann Hollweg on August 1, 1914, the day the Germans declared war on Russia.[22] Mitteleuropa assumed a central position in Bethmann Hollweg's September program and remained an important aim throughout the war.

On July 29 the chancellor assured the English ambassador that if England would declare neutrality in case of a German and Austro-Hungarian war against Russia and France, Germany would not threaten the territorial integrity of continental France or Belgium after the war. Bethmann Hollweg's offer suggested that these mutual assurances could serve as the basis of an Anglo-German neutrality agreement to be concluded after the war. This offer has been interpreted as evidence of Bethmann Hollweg's moderate intentions. But such an interpretation overlooks the fact that the German offer had two aspects. First, it was to guarantee England's neutrality for an extension of war into Russia, and second, it was to insure a German victory in the west. Bethmann Hollweg's promise to Goschen would have preserved the territorial integrity of France after her defeat, but in the absence of English opposition Germany would have had—and used—the opportunity to set her own terms. These "guarantees" would have forced France into dependence on Germany. Through the creation of a central European economic union, which would remove French export premiums, place French and German manufacturers on an equal basis in the acquisition of mine rights, standardize monopolies and direct and indirect tax laws, etc., the western European "theater" would have been eliminated from international competition; and, thanks to

21. I. Geiss, *Julikrise und Kriegsausbruch 1914*, vol. II (Hanover, 1964), nos. 684 and 745.
22. See the dissertation of J. Pragal.

the Anglo-German agreement, England would not have been able to wrest the "fruits of victory" from Germany. This was the objective of Bethmann Hollweg's offer.

In a letter of August 1, 1914, to the chancellor, Rathenau proposed this idea of exploiting victory over France —expected within four weeks—by establishing a central European economic area to include France. Bethmann Hollweg and his second-in-command, Minister of the Interior Delbrück, adopted the basic idea of this project during the first days of the war.[23] The Mitteleuropa plan was the central war aim Germany had developed to protect her position in western Europe. It was not a means of war, since it had been based on the assumption of Anglo-German cooperation well before England's opposition to Germany had become clear. A conversation between Bethmann Hollweg and his predecessor, Bülow, soon after the war began supports this interpretation. Bülow had been chosen to serve as a special ambassador to Italy, and his mission was to hold this Triple Alliance partner to its commitments.[24] In briefing Bülow, Bethmann Hollweg stated his belief that, after a quick German victory over France, England would mediate a peace that would create a cultural bloc in western Europe: Germany, England, and France against Muscovite Russia.

Bethmann Hollweg was a "Russophobe" and "Anglophile" by origin and tradition, and these tendencies made themselves felt in the policies of his chancellorship. The actions of the German "war chancellor" were not determined by a passive fatalism or a slow, indecisive, pessimistic nature but by the profound conviction that a war for continental primacy was not only inevitable but also necessary. Bethmann Hollweg, as well as the Kaiser, Moltke, and the

23. Deutsches Zentralarchiv, Potsdam, RK Grosses Hauptquartier, nos. 21 and 2476, Bethmann Hollweg to Delbrück, September 9, 1914, enclosure.
24. B. von Bülow, *Denkwürdigkeiten*, vol. III (Berlin, 1931), p. 148.

governmental departments, subscribed to the ideology of "a battle to the death between the Slavic and the Germanic peoples." The occasional quotes that Erdmann has released from Riezler's diary indicate how much the inevitable confrontation with the Russian colossus dominated the chancellor's thinking. But more specific material has been disclosed in personal papers only recently published.

This anti-Russian ideology was behind the demand to weaken Russia permanently by depriving her of the territory on her western border. Next to Mittelafrika, Asia Minor, and Mitteleuropa, this demand represented the most concrete war aim of the German government and nation. Bethmann Hollweg had introduced this goal in prewar propaganda, and he tried to realize it from the first day of war on. It had appeared in the curt opening phrases of his September program, drawn up when the collapse of France, the first step toward a new order in Europe, seemed imminent:

Securing Germany's position in the east and the west for all time. To this end, France must be so weakened that she cannot rise again as a great power; Russia must be pushed back from the German border as far as possible and her dominion over the non-Russian vassal peoples broken.[25]

"Protection and guarantee" of Germany's position and the opportunity for further "development" were German goals both before and during the war. Entry into the war did not bring any change in German policy; the geographical areas involved, the major thrusts, and the political maxims were the same. But now the war and expected victory seemed to have brought these goals within reach, and the resulting surge of optimism was reflected in a fiery rhetoric.

25. Deutsches Zentralarchiv, Potsdam, RK Grosses Hauptquartier, nos. 21 and 2476, Bethmann Hollweg to Delbrück, September 9, 1914, memorandum.

Only in this sense did the outbreak of war signify a change. It did not create any new goals, but it did raise hopes of realizing the old ones that had been pursued in vain through political and diplomatic means before the war. The war was felt as a liberation from the limits of the prewar order, not only in international politics but also in the economic and domestic realm. Indeed, the war was celebrated as a step toward Germany's becoming a cultural force destined for a mission of worldwide significance.

In September 1914, the *Süddeutsche Monatshefte*, encouraged by the government, published "an assessment of the nation by German and Austrian historians." It included contributions by Erich Marcks ("Bismarck and Our War"), Veit Valentin ("What We Have Aimed for since 1870"), Friedrich Meinecke ("Politics and Culture"), Hermann Oncken ("Germany and England"), Max Lenz ("The German God"), and Karl Alexander von Müller ("To Prussia"). Johannes Haller—whose history of Germany, published in 1919, colored the outlook of an entire generation, just as Treitschke's work did in his time—contributed a key article ("Thoughts of a Balt" [26]). This was essentially a public statement of the ideas of Wilhelm II, Bethmann Hollweg, and Jagow. "In order to make Russia harmless, her western provinces and especially her sea coasts must be taken from her, i.e., the territory of those 'non-Russian peoples' by whose conquest she participates in the life of Europe." Through the loss of "Finland, Lithuania, Poland, Little Russia, Bessarabia and the Black Sea coast, Russia will cease to be a major European power and will become again what she was before Peter the Great, when Leibniz could place her on a level with Persia and Abyssinia."

The Peace of Brest Litovsk was to achieve all these aims.

Haller continues: "If Russia were forced to cede those possessions which make her a mortal danger to us, then we

---

26. J. Haller, "Gedanken eines Balten," *Süddeutsche Monatshefte*, September 1914, pp. 812–16, especially pp. 815–16.

would finally be rid of the nightmare [Bethmann Hollweg's phrase from before and during the war] that haunted Frederick the Great in his time and that began so early to impair the growth of our new empire."

And as spokesman for the intellectual elite of 1914, Haller set the German "nation" this compelling task:

Let the German nation arise, strong and invincible, only in the greatest danger conscious of all her strength. Let her reclaim the place in the world that is hers, the place that she once had and that was taken from her in the ignoble times of her weakness. Let her be again what she was in days long gone— mistress of the north and east, champion of German culture, and safeguard of western civilization against the tyranny of Asiatic barbarism.

The July Crisis:
A Provocation to War

From the German point of view, the so-called July crisis was simply the logical conclusion of a planned diplomatic action. This diplomatic effort was to create a favorable alignment of the major powers for a continental war. German leaders were convinced this war was necessary, and the German people had been prepared for it.[1] The terms of European alliances and the interests of Germany's only ally, Austria-Hungary, dictated that the occasion for a continental war—the long awaited "reckoning" with France and Russia—arise from an Austro-Russian conflict in the Balkans.[2] German leaders were convinced that a general conflagration in the Balkans could be made to order at any

---

1. The final phase of the propaganda effort included the Russo-German press feud in March 1914 and the press articles about the Anglo-Russian negotiations on a naval convention. On this subject, see also the press files in my *Krieg der Illusionen*.
2. As Moltke said, "The attack must come from the Slavs." Moltke to Conrad, February 10, 1913, in F. Conrad von Hötzendorf, *Aus meiner Dienstzeit*, vol. III (Vienna, Leipzig, Berlin, 1962), p. 147.

time. As early as the spring of 1914, Conrad told the German ambassador to Vienna, Tschirschky, that "a threatening situation is always at hand in the Balkans"; [3] and in June 1914, von Stumm, director of the political section of the German Foreign Ministry, made a similar statement to the journalist Viktor Naumann, asserting that a war with Russia could develop overnight.[4] In June 1914, for example, the Albanian crisis, the expulsion of Prince Wied, or the impending war between Greece and Turkey could have been escalated into a European conflict. In short, there were incidents enough but as yet no event that would rouse the masses.

The assassination of the Austrian heir apparent on June 28, 1914, in Sarajevo provided the occasion for diplomatic measures leading to war, measures in which uncertainties could be reduced to a minimum. Most important, the Kaiser's reluctance to approve the war could be overcome, since he was sure to be outraged at the violation of the monarchical principle the "assassins of royalty" had committed. Secondly, doubts about Germany's ally Austria-Hungary could be put aside, since she would surely have to go along with Germany now. This might not have been the case if, for instance, war had broken out over the Albanian question. Thirdly, the question of unity among the German people was answered, particularly the question of the Social Democrats' attitude toward the war and their approval of war credits. The "people" stood united in "defense," and the entire Social Democratic Party seemed willing to "cooperate" in a war to shield Austria-Hungary from the dangers of Slavic autocracy and in the resulting struggle against the traditional enemy, France. The Archduke's death was a

---

3. Conrad, *Aus meiner Dienstzeit,* vol. III, p. 597: a "situation" in which one can do nothing but "get on with it"—even the indecisive Kaiser Wilhelm II.
4. *Österreich-Ungarns Aussenpolitik,* vol. VIII, no. 9966. Viktor Naumann, *Dokumente und Argumente,* pp. 5 f.

more likely cause for war than the two Albanian border cities of Dibra and Diakova. The Dual Monarchy would have gone to war over them the year before had she not been restrained by Germany. Finally, Germany cherished the not unfounded hope that at this stage England would remain neutral in a war caused by Slavic aggression.

Germany consciously exploited Sarajevo to further her world policy. To accomplish this, Germany had to use war or the serious threat of war to break up the Entente, which was perceived as an "encirclement" and represented as such in propaganda. The planned blitzkrieg against Serbia was a calculated provocation directed at Russia. If Russia accepted the challenge, Berlin hoped Germany could defeat Russia and France. But if Russia should unexpectedly retreat a third time, as in 1909 and 1912–13, abandoning Serbia, then Germany would "at least" have split the Entente and opened the way to the Balkans and the Ottoman Empire.

Thus, Bethmann Hollweg's allegedly passive fatalism turns out to be a consciously aggressive policy. He sought to exploit an apparently favorable opportunity to improve Germany's position in Europe, a position that was felt to be confining for Germany and her aspirations to power. In his book *Grundzüge der Weltpolitik* (*Fundamentals of World Politics*), published in 1914 under the pseudonym Ruedorffer, Riezler described Germany as being "crammed inside disadvantageous borders." [5]

Until recently, this interpretation of the July crisis met with furious criticism from Germany historians. I am grateful to Karl Dietrich Erdmann for publishing some excerpts from the Riezler diary,[6] because they confirm my interpre-

---

5. K. Riezler ("Ruedorffer"), *Grundzüge der Weltpolitik.* See, too, I. Geiss, *Deutschland vor dem Weltkrieg: Die Erforderlichkeit des Unmöglichen,* vol. II of the Hamburger Studien.

6. K. D. Erdmann, "Zur Beurteilung Bethmann Hollwegs," *Geschichte in Wissenschaft und Unterricht,* 15 (1964), pp. 525–40. Erdmann refused to let me see the Riezler diary.

tation and even carry it a step further. A case in point is Bethmann Hollweg's statement made at Hohenfinow on July 8, two days after the German government had agreed to support Austria-Hungary: "If war does not materialize —if the Tsar does not want it or if France in her dismay recommends peace—we at least have a chance to split the Entente over this issue." [7]

Erdmann has confirmed still another of my points that was vehemently attacked by my critics, i.e., the connection between Germany's world policy and her continental policy. He speaks of Germany's desire "to establish political, military, and economic fronts to the east and west of the Empire." [8] Bethmann Hollweg's young friend Riezler expressed this demand in his book when he urged making "Germany so strong on the continent that she stands to win against any possible combination of powers." He added: "The fate of German world policy will be decided on the continent." [9]

If we consider Germany's behavior in the July crisis in the light of her policy during the last years of peace—and we must consider it this way historically—then we see that Germany was determined to accept what seemed "inevitable and imminent," [10] a violent confrontation with the ever more threatening Russian colossus and its financial backer, France.

On December 10, 1913, Kaiser Wilhelm II and Moltke had told King Albert of Belgium: "La guerre est inévitable et plus prochaine que vous ne le croyez." [11] The confronta-

---

7. *Ibid.*, p. 536.
8. *Ibid.*, p. 539. K. D. Erdmann, *Die Zeit*, September 25, 1964.
9. Riezler, *Grundzüge der Weltpolitik*, pp. 106 f.
10. Moltke to Melotte, the Belgian military attaché in Berlin, November 6, 1913; secret report of H. de Melotte to the Belgian Minister of War, de Broqueville, November 29, 1913, in the collection of Dr. Jenni.
11. *French Orange Book*, August 1914, no. 6; Beyens, *L'Allemagne avant la guerre* (Brussels and Paris, 1915), pp. 24–26; R. Poincaré, *Memoiren*, vol. II (Dresden, 1928), pp. 183–85.

tion with Russia had been seen for years as a "battle to the death between Germans and Slavs," "a decisive struggle between the races." The Kaiser, Jagow, Moltke, Karl Lamprecht, Riezler, and, somewhat more cautiously, Bethmann Hollweg spoke in these terms.[12] A German white book of August 2, 1914, says that "the collapse of Austria and the subjection of all the Slavic peoples to the Russian scepter would make the position of the German race in Europe untenable." [13] From the beginning, the war was seen in the exaggerated ideological terms of a racial conflict, a view shared by Bethmann Hollweg.

The burning question for German statesmen was what position England would take in this continental conflict.[14] Since 1909, Bethmann Hollweg had sought to insure English neutrality should Germany "get involved" in a continental war. On February 10, 1913, when Austria wanted to start a preventive war against Serbia, Bethmann Hollweg had warned Berchtold against the use of force at this point. Bethmann Hollweg considered it "a grave mistake to force . . . a solution when we have the prospect—however distant—of resolving the conflict under more favorable conditions." He believed there were ". . . various indications" suggesting "that Entente policy is on the decline," and that "a new orientation of English policy" was imminent.[15] In February 1913, the German chancellor and his foreign policy staff knew that an Austro-Hungarian military action against Serbia would lead to the immediate intervention of Russia and consequently to world war. Why

---

12. F. Fischer, *Griff nach der Weltmacht*, pp. 40 f. *et passim* for Wilhelm II and Moltke. See also the references in *Krieg der Illusionen*.

13. I. Geiss, *Julikrise und Kriegsausbruch 1914*, vol. II, no. 1089, p. 639.

14. F. Fischer, *Griff nach der Weltmacht*, pp. 39 f.

15. *Grosse Politik*, vol. XXXIV, I, no. 12818, Bethmann Hollweg to Berchtold. See also H. Hantsch, *Berchtold*, vol. I, pp. 387 f., who quotes the letter of Bethmann Hollweg from Franz Ferdinand's papers.

should Bethmann Hollweg have forgotten that in July 1914?

In the summer of 1914, the "more favorable conditions" seemed to be at hand. Two major factors helped provide these conditions: first, the Anglo-German agreements concerning the Portuguese colonies and the Baghdad railroad; and second, the psychologically and morally favorable climate of opinion created by the assassination at Sarajevo.

My critics have recently held up to me Bethmann Hollweg's few statements which supposedly demonstrate that he —like Moltke and the Kaiser—expected England to support Russia and France. But these statements cannot change the copiously documented fact that the chancellor thought he could negotiate English neutrality in the impending continental war. At the least, he hoped to prevent England's immediate entry and thus to assure German victory over France. Only from this perspective are Bethmann Hollweg's efforts, his anxiety, dismay, and eventual despair over England's actions understandable. But England could act as he hoped only if the provocation for war appeared to come from Russia and France.[16] Indeed, the more Bethmann Hollweg was forced to realize that England's neutrality and her mediating efforts were closely linked, the more it became the *ultima ratio* of his policy to convince England, the German people, and history that Russia was the villain of the piece. If it is true that he had reckoned on England as a third opponent from the beginning—as Erdmann and Zechlin claim, going a step further than I—then his policy seems even more of a gamble. But this increased risk of war has little effect on my interpretation of the July

16. Bethmann Hollweg to Kaiser Wilhelm II, December 18, 1912, Auswärtiges Amt Bonn, England 78, vol. 31; Bethmann Hollweg to Lerchenfeld, June 9, 1914, and Lerchenfeld to Hertling, June 4, 1914, Dirr. no. 1. Moltke expressed similar thoughts to Conrad, February 10, 1913, Conrad, *Aus meiner Dienstzeit,* vol. III, p. 147.

crisis. Even if Bethmann Hollweg had reckoned on the entry of England (the evidence which the Riezler diary has so far yielded cannot be evaluated without the context in which it occurs), his actions and attitude show that he was bent on neutralizing her and felt certain he could do so. But Bethmann Hollweg did not really know what England would do if Belgium were invaded. He was anxious about England's reaction, not, as Erdmann and Zechlin claim, about the fact of war itself. My critics insist that Bethmann Hollweg reckoned on English participation in a continental war from the outset. They do so to argue in turn that the magnitude of the risk taken—war against three opponents —shows the magnitude of the threat to Germany. But that view is obviously shortsighted because it deliberately fails to ask whose words and deeds during the past two decades had brought Germany to the point of feeling threatened.

Erdmann and Zechlin base their argument on a fragmentary quotation from the Riezler diary: "action a leap in the dark, and this leap the gravest duty . . ." [17] A profound aphorism, a Delphic pronouncement. Any interpretation is possible, or none at all, as long as the Riezler diary is not open to scholars. Until it is, I would say only this: "action" (not "war") apparently means the military confrontation with France and Russia. Because England's position was uncertain, it was impossible to predict the course of such a conflict—in contrast to that of a cabinet war—or even to make complete plans for its initial phase. Hence "a leap in the dark." The decision was a "duty" because it could further German interests, but it was also "grave" because it involved considerable risk. We see then how a document cited to prove that Germany counted England among her certain opponents from the start might instead demonstrate uncertainty, i.e., that German leaders were still hoping for En-

17. K. D. Erdmann, *Geschichte in Wissenschaft und Unterricht,* p. 536, from the Riezler diary, entry of July 14, 1914.

glish neutrality. Until sources not presently available prove my interpretation wrong, I consider it valid.[18]

My critics make use of another indirect quotation from the Riezler diary, which states that "in the event of war, an English attempt to land in Pomerania is a very real possibility." [19] Without knowledge of the wording and context I cannot judge how "real" Bethmann Hollweg considered this possibility. For the present, though, I am doubtful about serious expectations of this kind since the Siebert reports, Bethmann Hollweg's source of information, contain nothing about such a British plan. In the protocol of a Russian naval staff meeting of May 26, included in these reports, there is only a *Russian* suggestion of using English merchant ships to make up for the shortage of Russian transport ships for a *Russian* landing in Pomerania.[20] But the English admiralty staff did not pick up this suggestion.

Thirdly, in evaluating the decisions made in the July crisis, Zechlin in particular attributes great importance to "strained Anglo-German relations" resulting from Anglo-Russian negotiations toward a naval agreement. According to Zechlin, Bethmann Hollweg knew "that England and Russia were already planning coordinated operations in the North and Baltic Seas." [21] Since Zechlin gives no documentation to support this claim, I cannot surmise from what "secret source" Bethmann Hollweg could have obtained this knowledge. Nothing to this effect appears in the corre-

---

18. Erdmann has informed me that he has published "everything important" from the diary. But I believe that no historical conclusions can be reached on the basis of this fragmentary hodgepodge of quotations, nor can any be reached unless the individual historian himself can look into the entire body of material available.

19. K. D. Erdmann, *Geschichte in Wissenschaft und Unterricht,* p. 536.

20. B. von Siebert, *Diplomatische Aktenstücke zur Geschichte der Ententepolitik der Vorkriegsjahre,* vol. II (Berlin and Leipzig, 1925), enclosure to Sasanov's letter to Benckendorff, May 28, 1914, p. 819.

21. E. Zechlin, *Geschichte in Wissenschaft und Unterricht,* 16, p. 73.

spondence of the Russian embassy in London, made available by Siebert. The most concrete formulation occurs in the protocol of the Russian naval staff meeting of May 26 mentioned above: "It was recognized that the main objective of our naval agreement with England—like that of the Franco-Russian one—should be to organize coordinated but independent operations for the respective navies." And later in the same protocol we find still another Russian idea that London had not accepted and never would: "Operations in the Baltic and North Seas and those in the Mediterranean must be considered as separate entities." [22]

Negotiations on the naval agreement were by no means as far advanced in June 1914 as Zechlin claims they were. Joint discussions had been planned, but on June 25, because of news leaks originating in the German foreign office, Grey postponed the beginning of these negotiations to a later, quieter time.[23] Germany had been able to block the negotiations. Nothing in this incident proves that England would have entered the war immediately. But the Germans might well have concluded that it was high time to act, since the naval negotiations were clearly a response to Germany's overbearing actions in the spring of 1914. England had not committed herself yet. Indeed, Grey and the English government had again accommodated the Germans. But how much longer would they? Were not the fruits of Anglo-German cooperation ripe—perhaps overripe? Had not Germany's behavior in the spring of 1914 given the English a hint of why the Germans were anxious for an understanding with Downing Street?

English neutrality was the point on which German policy hinged. To insure English neutrality, it was essential that Austria-Hungary draw Russia into war with a blitzkrieg in

22. Siebert, vol. II, pp. 818, 819.
23. A. Bach, "Die englisch-russischen Verhandlungen von 1914 über den Abschluss einer Marinekonvention," *Preussische Jahrbücher,* vol. 197 (1924), p. 188.

the Balkans. Only then would Germany get the war she wanted; only then would the way be open for war against France and Russia. This is why Germany wanted a blitzkrieg and why she urged Vienna to act immediately. If Vienna hesitated, the German Foreign Ministry would find itself in the awkward situation of having to parry the questions and the mediatory efforts of the other European powers without betraying Germany's own desire for war. But what Berlin feared did in fact happen. Valuable time was lost because Vienna decided, influenced by international law and moral considerations, to precede its punitive war against Serbia with the diplomatic action of an unacceptable ultimatum.[24] The resulting delay and the additional delay of actual military operations after the Austro-Hungarian declaration of war on Serbia caused German policy still further embarrassment. Germany had "to see the thing through" and play innocent by summoning all possible diplomatic finesse and deception. It was during this period that both Jagow and Bethmann Hollweg showed their skill. No better reflections of Germany's attitude in July 1914 can be cited than Jagow's "communiqués" and "revisions."

Russia's unexpected restraint, her willingness to negotiate, threw off German calculations more than anything else. Presenting Russia as the aggressor became increasingly difficult because Russia had not announced general mobilization. This made the possibility of English neutrality even more unlikely, and growing uncertainty about England's plans explains what Ritter calls an "unfortunate" [25] inquiry about her neutrality that Bethmann Hollweg addressed to Goschen on the evening of June 29.[26] This inquiry could

24. I. Geiss, *Julikrise und Kriegsausbruch 1914,* vol. I, no. 39, Austro-Hungarian Ministerial Council meeting, July 7, 1914.
25. G. Ritter, *Staatskunst und Kriegshandwerk: Das Problem des "Militarismus" in Deutschland,* vol. II: *Die Hauptmächte Europas und das Wilhelminische Reich (1890–1914)* (Munich, 1960), p. 319.
26. I. Geiss, *Julikrise und Kriegsausbruch 1914,* vol. II, nos. 684, 745.

better be called ill-timed, because it revealed Germany's determination to go to war just after a telegram had arrived from the German ambassador in London indicating that England would enter the war immediately if Germany attacked France or Belgium.[27]

During that night and the following two days, Bethmann Hollweg urged the Austro-Hungarian government to respond to England's efforts at mediation: Vienna should resume direct Austro-Russian talks and accept the suggestion to halt in Belgrade. It was not Bethmann Hollweg's intention at all to prevent war but rather to salvage what he could of the bankrupt legacy of his prewar diplomacy. He assumed that it would be impossible for Grey to intervene *immediately* in a continental war provoked by Russian mobilization. Expecting his efforts to succeed, Bethmann Hollweg was able to resist pressure from the military to announce German mobilization. He pointed out to them that it was politically essential for Russia to mobilize first.[28] The chancellor alone remained cool in the hectic atmosphere. His policy was determined not only by the question of English neutrality but also by the desire to make it easier for the Social Democratic leaders to approve war credits. He knew the Social Democrats would accept only a defensive war to stem an attack by tsarist Russia. They would agree to war with France reluctantly and only if France came to the aid of her Russian ally.

Bethmann Hollweg's plan succeeded on the domestic front, but it was a failure in terms of foreign policy. In a speech given in the Reichstag on August 4, he had emphasized Anglo-German efforts for peace, but only a few hours later he received England's ultimatum.[29] Close Anglo-German cooperation had been stressed as late as the German

27. *Ibid.,* no. 678.
28. *Ibid.,* no. 676.
29. *Ibid.,* nos. 1156, 1158; *British Documents,* vol. XI, no. 671.

white book of August 2: "Shoulder to shoulder with England we have worked incessantly to mediate . . ." [30]

Even after England had declared war, Bethmann Hollweg did not relinquish his goals entirely. As the conversation with Bülow, mentioned above, and several talks with Tirpitz in August 1914 show, Bethmann Hollweg hoped to end the first phase of military operations so quickly that England would not be able to prevent French defeat. Here, as in other instances, he was inspired by the compelling example of Prussian national history in the year 1866. He was certain that after the defeat of France the German negotiating position with England would be unassailable and that England would have to "come around," as it was put in the prewar period. [31] After all his original hopes had proved illusory, Bethmann Hollweg still wanted to delay English intervention. The Germans still hoped to be home again "when the leaves fall."

Despite the failure with England, the victorious advance of the German army at the end of August and beginning of September seemed to bear out German calculations made during the July crisis. The Germans expected victory over France, a victory England was unable to prevent. They hoped that military confrontation with England would now become superfluous. In any case, victory over France would put Germany in a favorable position for the second Punic War that Wilhelm II anticipated in the fall of 1914. England would have to recognize this shift in the balance of power on the continent. In the consciousness of the German nation, victory over Russia would now be possible, even though the war had not begun as expected.

30. I. Geiss, *Julikrise und Kriegsausbruch 1914,* vol. II, no. 1089, p. 642.
31. *Der Kaiser . . .* , ed. W. Görlitz, p. 119.

The September Program:
Not an Insignificant
Interlude but a Blueprint
for World Power

In numerous articles,[1] Egmont Zechlin has developed the theory that after "concluding the border battles of the first phase" Bethmann Hollweg wanted to effect a change in English policy "to guarantee Germany's gains in power." According to Zechlin, even if "the limited war" escalated from a local Balkan conflict to a continental war and finally to a great European war involving England, "it was to be prevented from developing into a hegemonic struggle that would have to be fought to the end." [2] If we look behind the verbal obfuscation here and reduce this interpretation to its basic assumptions, the argument proves to be nothing but old wine in new bottles. Zechlin is merely adding a new

1. E. Zechlin, "Deutschland zwischen Kabinettskrieg und Wirtschaftskrieg," *Historische Zeitschrift,* 199/2 (October 1964), pp. 347–458; E. Zechlin, "Probleme des Kriegskalküls und der Kriegsbeendigung im ersten Weltkrieg," *Geschichte in Wissenschaft und Unterricht,* 16/2 (1965), pp. 69–83; E. Zechlin, *Die Zeit,* October 9, 1964.
2. E. Zechlin, *Historische Zeitschrift,* 199/2, p. 362.

twist to the assertion of older German historiography [3] that England was primarily responsible for the First *World* War. Traditional German scholarship held England responsible because England could not or would not restrain Russian Pan-Slavism from an aggressive war. Now, Zechlin shifts the claim of English guilt from July to September 1914. According to Zechlin, Germany was forced to fight for survival when England, by her decision to conduct war *"à outrance,"* [4] altered the nature of Germany's limited war, or, as Zechlin says, converted a "cabinet war into an economically motivated hegemonic struggle." [5]

This interpretation violates historical truth. In the minds of German leaders the war against Russia and France had always been a struggle for hegemony. One need think only of the Kaiser's numerous marginalia about "war to the death between Germans and Gallo-Russians" to see that German prewar thinking allows only one interpretation of the war begun in August 1914. By eliminating France and Russia as independent powers, Germany hoped to achieve hegemony and thus insure her own position of power "for all time."

Zechlin accuses me of imposing a "concrete analysis of motive" onto the "logical analysis of function" in Ludwig Dehio's interpretation of the First World War. Dehio writes: "Only then [during the war] did we assume the function of a European hegemonic power." [6] My interpretation is supposedly based on "preconceived notions." [7] The fact is that Germany developed the policy goal of "hegemony in

3. E.g., E. Anrich, *Die englische Politik im Juli 1914: Eine Gesamtdarstellung der Julikrise* (Stuttgart and Berlin, 1934). The Wissenschaftliche Buchgesellschaft of Darmstadt republished this book in 1965 and offered it to subscribers!
4. E. Zechlin, *Historische Zeitschrift*, 199/2, p. 419.
5. *Ibid.*
6. L. Dehio, *Deutschland und die Weltpolitik im 20. Jahrhundert*, 1961, p. 16.
7. E. Zechlin, *Historische Zeitschrift*, 199/2, p. 363.

Europe" [8] long before the war, not during it. "Analysis of function" and "analysis of motive" stand in a dialectical relationship and interact with each other, particularly in the continuity of prewar and wartime policy that I have traced. Zechlin's "analysis of motive" unfortunately lacks all documentation, and his separation of "analysis of motive" and "analysis of function" is invalid. But it is clear to me how necessary this separation is for his interpretation of a "planned" cabinet war and an "unwanted" war for hegemony. Only in this way can he present an analysis that goes against the sources. Here, indeed, "preconceived notions determine the interpretation of historical events."

Zechlin had to construct his thesis after I published the September program in 1961. This document had been known to German historians since 1942.[9] On September 9, 1914, at the apparent high point of German military success, Bethmann Hollweg sent this program from military headquarters in Luxemburg to his second-in-command in Berlin, Clemens Delbrück, Minister of the Interior and Vice-Chancellor.[10] Here Bethmann Hollweg lay down guidelines for "establishing a German peace" after victory. He dealt with what I consider the crucial question: what shape should Europe take after a German victory, a victory which every German expected [11] and about which, after it had not been won, hundreds of works were written, pro-

---

8. Dehio, p. 16.
9. Information from the register of document users in the former Imperial Archives.
10. Deutsches Zentralarchiv, I, RK 2476, Bethmann Hollweg to Delbrück, September 9, 1914.
11. As an example among many, see the collection *Deutsche Reden in schwerer Zeit,* Berlin, 1914, which includes speeches by U. von Wilamowitz-Moellendorf, G. Roethe, H. Delbrück, O. von Giercke, A. Lasson, A. von Harnack, M. Sering, and F. von Liszt, among others. See also Bethmann Hollweg's speech to the Reichstag, August 4, 1914, in *Kriegsrundschau,* vol. I, nos. 1–30 (Berlin, 1915), pp. 67 ff. See also AA WK Grosses Hauptquartier 21, vol. I, Zimmermann to Bethmann Hollweg, September 9, 1914.

pounding how it could have been won. But this expectation of victory, indeed this obsession with victory—although it has no bearing on whether Germany was responsible for the war or had it "forced upon" her—is what German historians in 1964 deny.[12] In their view, Bethmann Hollweg was convinced that Germany should not win because, as the "first defeatist" of his nation, he feared that a military victory would mean the defeat of the German spirit.[13] For this reason, German historians contend, he did not want to win.

However one chooses to interpret the qualms Bethmann Hollweg expressed in January 1918 in a letter to Prince Max of Baden, an assessment of the chancellor must be based primarily on the plentiful evidence of his public statements and of his statements in the official records. These documents make it clear that Bethmann Hollweg consciously regarded himself as the spokesman of the "nation" and of the German will to victory.[14] This man, whom Zechlin presents as a near-socialist, saw "the German Reich and particularly the Prussian state," built on "the firm foundation" of "dedication to the state and to the political system the Social Democrats have habitually branded as militarism." As Bethmann Hollweg said on September 19, he was ready to consider a "reorientation" of German domestic policy only when "the German Left is prepared to support the idea of a nation in arms and to accept the national

12. See E. Zechlin, *Historische Zeitschrift*, 199/2, pp. 369 f.; E. Zechlin, *Geschichte in Wissenschaft und Unterricht*, 16, pp. 74 ff.; and the works of Erdmann, Hölzle, Steglich, Engels, and Herzfeld.
13. See E. Zechlin, *Historische Zeitschrift*, 199/2, pp. 355 ff. and 451 ff. for Bethmann Hollweg's letter to Max of Baden, January 17, 1918. For K. D. Erdmann's judgment of Bethmann Hollweg, see *Geschichte in Wissenschaft und Unterricht*, 15, pp. 527, 529 ff., and especially 538 ff.
14. See, for example, the documents dealing with the American mediation efforts in the AA WK Grosses Hauptquartier 21, vol. I; Zimmermann to Bethmann Hollweg, September 9, 1914, and Bethmann Hollweg to Zimmermann, September 12, 1914. See also the speeches of Bethmann Hollweg in the Reichstag on August 4, 1914.

spirit behind it." [15] Is this a man who was reluctant to accept victory? As chancellor of the German people, he was the people's chancellor only as long as the nation felt he represented Germany's desire for power and her efforts to achieve it.

There are two ways to minimize the political importance of the September program: one is Ritter's; the other is Zechlin's. Ritter presents the program as a temporary concession Bethmann Hollweg made, although his own thinking had suddenly taken a different turn. It was a concession to the "longings and the patriotic dreams of a people at war" [16] (or of the journalists and politicians who created "public opinion"). Ritter sees the September program as the result of an excusable and temporary weakness, of a national passion. But when it cannot be denied that other German politicians made the same or similar demands, Ritter disqualifies these men as "opportunists" (e.g., Erzberger,[17] who acted as spokesman of industrial groups [18]) or even as "Pan-Germans" (e.g., Bassermann and Stresemann [19]). For Ritter, German war aims are the "annexationist dreams of German patriots." Where he cannot deny demands actually made in the September program (like the annexation of Longwy-Briey), he minimizes their significance, disregarding historical fact. Bethmann Hollweg held to the demand for annexation of Longwy-Briey almost until he left office in July 1917. Ritter claims that Bethmann Hollweg "regarded this annexation as no great imposition, because France possessed sufficient ore deposits in Normandy and because the mines of Briey were, for the

15. Deutsches Zentralarchiv, Potsdam, RK Grosses Hauptquartier 21, no. 2476, Bethmann Hollweg to Delbrück, September 19, 1914.
16. G. Ritter, *Staatskunst und Kriegshandwerk,* vol. III: *Die Tragödie der Staatskunst: Bethmann Hollweg als Kriegskanzler 1914–1917* (Munich, 1964), p. 21.
17. *Ibid.,* p. 36.
18. F. Fischer, *Griff nach der Weltmacht,* pp. 131 f.
19. G. Ritter, *Staatskunst und Kriegshandwerk,* vol. III, p. 178 for Bassermann, p. 50 for Stresemann; see also p. 592.

most part, already in German hands before the war." [20]
This conclusion borders on the cynical. Ritter fails to mention that as early as 1913, in discussions with the Italian Minister of Commerce, Nitti, spokesmen of German heavy industry named Longwy-Briey as a war aim.[21] He further ignores how crucial the Briey ore deposits were to the existence of French industry and to the position of France as an industrial nation. The innumerable memoranda, proposals, reports, and statistics (originating in the German Ministry of the Interior, for the most part) testify to the importance of the deposits.[22] An influential memorandum from the Ministry of the Interior concluded: "The loss of French Lorraine would, for all practical purposes, mean the end of French heavy industry. The importance the acquisition of this area would have for Germany can hardly be exaggerated. . . . France would lose nine tenths of her present ore production and, although ore deposits may also exist in Normandy and Brittany, . . . they have been only partially located and explored." [23] For Ritter these reports are only bureaucratic busy work and had no influence on the chief executive's decision.[24]

Ritter's interpretation of plans for handling the "Belgian problem" also tries to extenuate and "empathize." [25] In the

20. *Ibid.,* p. 45.
21. F. Nitti, *Das friedlose Europa,* 2nd ed. (Frankfurt am Main, no date), p. 23.
22. Deutsches Zentralarchiv, Potsdam, RdI 5, Erzgebiet von Longwy-Briey, vol. I, no. 19305. RWA, Wirtschaftliche Verhandlungen in den besetzten Gebieten, 2 Frankreich, no. 876/1; RWA, Friedensverhandlungen mit Frankreich, March 1915–November 1918, no. 1883, and Brieybecken, no. 1884; RK Krieg 15, vol. I, no. 2442/10; Auswärtiges Amt Bonn, WK 20b, vol. I: Zukunft der besetzten Gebiete Frankreich. On this whole question, see F. Fischer, *Griff nach der Weltmacht,* pp. 332 ff. and 808 ff.
23. Deutsches Zentralarchiv, Potsdam, RWA 3, Frieden Frankreich, gen. vol. I, no. 1883: Memorandum of March 10, 1915, "Zur Frage des Erwerbs des französisch-lothringischen Erzgebietes" (by Schoenebeck).
24. As at the Historical Convention in Berlin during October 1964.
25. G. Ritter, *Staatskunst und Kriegshandwerk,* vol. III, p. 45.

September program and in statements made during the same period, Belgium is always referred to as a future tributary or vassal state.[26]

Ritter writes: "Bethmann Hollweg wanted neither the annexation of Belgium nor the re-establishment of the *status quo ante bellum*. He (like everyone [!] at that time, even the fundamentally anti-annexationist minister, von Loebell) only [!] wanted access to France through Belgium." [27] What did this "only" mean? It would have meant forcing Belgium to destroy her fortifications, to grant German troops the right of occupation and passage, to place her harbors—especially Antwerp—at German disposal, and to cede Liège to Germany. It would also have meant exploiting this powerless Belgium as a base of operations for controlling the French canal ports of Dunkirk, Calais, and Boulogne, and thus for maintaining access to France from the north. "Only" means nothing more nor less than this.

On November 10, 1914, Bethmann Hollweg said to the Württemberg prime minister, Weizsäcker: "Belgium is a frightful problem." For Ritter, this is reason enough to claim that "the unsolved 'Belgian question' (in the last analysis an unhappy legacy of the ill-fated [!] 'Schlieffen plan')" had "become the curse of Germany's entire war policy." That settles the matter for Ritter. It is the "legacy of the ill-fated Schlieffen plan" that poses a problem for him, not Germany's will to power and her desire to achieve power. For him, the declared determination of the German government and of German economic leaders never to allow Belgium to emerge again as a completely sovereign and independent state is not a planned program, not the conscious, calculated pursuit of a goal. Ritter prefers to speak of a "curse." [28]

Ritter also deliberately overlooks Germany's fierce and

26. F. Fischer, *Griff nach der Weltmacht*, p. 135 ff.
27. G. Ritter, *Staatskunst und Kriegshandwerk*, vol. III, p. 45.
28. G. Ritter, in *Festschrift P. E. Schramm*, 1964, p. 208.

single-minded determination to realize the Mitteleuropa program. Admittedly, this plan was modified to suit the changing military situation, but its basic intent as an instrument of German domination was never altered. Ritter goes so far as to say only that the Mitteleuropa plan was "the truly original and surprising element in Bethmann Hollweg's war aims program." But how can this aim be ascribed to Bethmann Hollweg alone?

Zechlin provides another method of minimizing the importance of the September program. He obscures and plays down the clear intent of the program, which, apart from its origins in prewar policy, evolved in top-level discussions from the *first* day of the war on.[29] He does this by dwelling on secondary negotiations and events. For example, to make Bethmann Hollweg's assessment of the English desire for war plausible, he indignantly cites the "disregard for international law" that English confiscation of German private property represented in the eyes of German leaders.[30] It is astonishing that Zechlin should call attention to this "disregard for international law," since both Germany's invasion of Belgium and her actions there were a violation of international law that shocked England and the entire world. But it should not surprise us that Zechlin cannot document his claim that England's "disregard for international law" affected Bethmann Hollweg's assessment of her position.

Zechlin's interpretation also takes economic aspects of the war into account. Drawing on remarks made by Gwinner, Rathenau, and Ballin, he claims that Germany expected England to experience a war boom and therefore to be interested in prolonging the war.[31] But Zechlin does not quote Gwinner fully. Gwinner does say that England will

---

29. C. von Delbrück, *Mobilmachung* (Munich, 1924), pp. 124 f. See, too, the dissertation of my student J. Pragal.
30. E. Zechlin, *Historische Zeitschrift,* 199/2, pp. 364 ff.
31. *Ibid.,* pp. 386 ff.

experience a war boom, but he doubts "that this will be recognized by the English soon enough to affect their decision
on the length of the war." [32] In addition to Tirpitz's observations in *Deutsche Ohnmachtspolitik im 1. Weltkrieg* (*Germany's Policy of Weakness in the First World War*), Zechlin
cites the notes and letters of the anti-British chief of the
naval staff, Pohl, as proof of Bethmann Hollweg's "change
of course." [33] According to Zechlin, this change occurred
between August 27 and September 4, 1914.[34]

In Zechlin's rendering of Pohl, news of the "dispatch of
Japanese troops to the European theatre" [35] is supposed to
have "visibly disquieted" Bethmann Hollweg. Pohl "reas-
sured" the chancellor with a remark which Zechlin, in his
usual fashion, fails to quote: "I [Pohl] am doing my best to
reassure him [Bethmann Hollweg], because I consider this
[the sending of Japanese troops to Europe] unlikely.
Japan needs at least four weeks to prepare and mobilize,
and the trip by sea would require ten weeks." [36] The German General Staff, the government, and the whole "nation"
believed victory in the west would be won long before this
period had elapsed.

Pohl also expected rapid victory and English readiness to
make peace. He was convinced that "the war is hurting England enormously. She lacks not only food but also raw
materials and markets, e.g., Germany. England cannot
withstand this pressure over an extended period and will try
to make peace. *We must force her to continue the war.*" [37]
Comparison of Pohl's complete statement (to which

---

32. A. von Tirpitz, *Deutsche Ohnmachtspolitik im 1. Weltkrieg* (Hamburg
    and Berlin, 1925), pp. 65 ff., on a conversation between Capelle and
    Gwinner, August 22, 1914.
33. E. Zechlin, *Historische Zeitschrift*, 199/2, p. 393.
34. *Ibid.*, p. 361.
35. *Ibid.*, p. 393.
36. H. Pohl, *Aus Aufzeichnungen und Briefen während der Kriegszeit*,
    Berlin, 1920, pp. 46 ff., entry of September 4, 1914.
37. *Ibid.*, conversation between Bethmann Hollweg and Pohl, August
    18, 1914, in Koblenz, p. 17. My italics.

Bethmann Hollweg certainly did not subscribe) with Zechlin's account provides another example of Zechlin's use of
sources. In his argument, Zechlin cites a letter that Pohl
wrote to his wife on September 5, but this letter expresses
nothing more than Pohl's regret "that we in the navy can
do nothing at all, *while the army advances from victory to
victory.* The English fleet is too strong for us." Pohl is
grateful that Bethmann Hollweg and Jagow "recognized
how difficult this situation was for the navy" and were even
willing "to continue the build-up of the navy." Bethmann
Hollweg's assertion "that England's envy and animosity toward our people caused the war and that she was bent on
crushing the rising competitor" [38] (a claim Tirpitz "still"
could not believe) only partially explains Bethmann Hollweg's plans for the navy. They must be seen primarily in
the context of another statement of the same day, in which
he explained why he did not deploy the fleet: ". . . the
fleet must be held in reserve to prevent England from depriving us of the *rewards of victory over France and
Russia.*" [39] This central statement suggests that once victory
in the west was won (and on September 5—that is, before
the Marne—Bethmann Hollweg certainly expected it to be)
the chancellor wanted to make Germany's "rewards of victory" safe from England and to create "assurances" of German dominance in the west. Bethmann Hollweg's statement
does not reflect his awareness, his "shattering realization,"
that England was an unconquerable opponent who gained
by the war and therefore wanted to prolong it. Instead, it
reflects his certainty of German victory in the west, a victory that would "secure Germany's position in the east and
in the west for all time."

A report of the military plenipotentiary of Württemberg,
von Graevenitz, expresses this same certainty of victory. On
the basis of many discussions at military headquarters, he

---

38. *Ibid.,* p. 50, letter of Pohl to his wife, September 5, 1914.
39. *Ibid.,* p. 49, Pohl's entry of September 5, 1914.

reported that the government wanted to take enough money from France and Belgium to allow an enormous increase of the German fleet. A memorandum from the parties of the Right urged this increase on the chancellor.[40] Like Bethmann Hollweg, the leaders of these parties felt this was the only way to defeat England and Japan, whether now or later.[41]

The fact that a proclamation from the Kaiser to the French people was drafted on September 5 is another clear sign that Germany expected rapid victory. The proclamation was not published because of the German defeat at the Marne, and it does not indicate the actual terms of a future peace. It was, after all, the draft of a proclamation. But it would have informed the French population that Germany planned to occupy at least northern France until "England allowed the French government to conclude peace." Zechlin dwells on aspects of the proclamation designed to appeal to French property owners, stressing German assurances of respect for private property. He asserts that German actions were based on "respect for France and a desire to protect her." [42] But he does not say that France was supposed to serve as Germany's financeer and military glacis, and he fails to mention the assumption of victory over France behind all these ideas. Victory was the German objective. Victory would mark the end of France as a great power and would reduce her to a German tributary state. The September program, completed at this time, states this objective unequivocally.

In the vocabulary of the imperialistic period "peace" has a purely pragmatic meaning. It did not suggest the "renunciation" of a "free hand" by a power at war. For Germany

40. Tirpitz, *Deutsche Ohnmachtspolitik,* pp. 94 f., statement of September 5, 1914.
41. E. Zechlin, *Geschichte in Wissenschaft und Unterricht,* 16, p. 77, Graevenitz to C. von Weizsäcker, September 5, 1914.
42. E. Zechlin, *Historische Zeitschrift,* 199/2, pp. 376 ff. and 362 ff.; cf. Deutsches Zentralarchiv I, RK no. 2465/1.

"peace" meant "insuring" her position of power. There would be no peace in Germany's terms until a unity of economic, military, political, and party interests had been achieved. Her war aims policy of 1914 to 1918 shows what that meant. Zechlin's exaggeration of moral and international considerations and his model of "limited war" play down the importance of Germany's desire for power and completely misunderstand the Wilhelminian state's determination to control the seas and take its "place in the sun." This state had no qualms about violating international law in August 1914. It felt free to use the idolized sword not only to negotiate a peace with England but also to win its place in the east, the west, and overseas. The September program was a plan for world power. The terms for securing this power varied with Germany's fortunes in the war, reflecting her hopes of victory and her disappointments in defeat. The plan was not to be followed to the letter, but it did bring the demands and dynamics of Germany to a focus. It was a clear and comprehensible outline, an alternative to goals of limited domination, an incentive to counteract defeatist *status quo* thinking. Despite all crises, the September program continued to reflect the geopolitical aspirations of the central power of Europe.

But according to Zechlin, Bethmann Hollweg resorted to this program as a defensive measure only after the German offer to leave England's position of power unimpaired was rejected. A succession of "breaches of confidence" with England forced Germany to prepare for a hegemonic struggle. Zechlin presents the program as no more than this: a preparation for hegemonic war forced on Germany by England. It was therefore not a war aim but only a strategic measure, and according to Zechlin, it was seriously considered for only a few days.[43] Thus, for Zechlin, the program was not a formulation of Germany's desire to change the balance of

43. E. Zechlin, *Historische Zeitschrift,* 199/2, pp. 429 ff.

power in Europe and in the world. It was instead an act of desperation on the part of Bethmann Hollweg, who had been disappointed by England and who—after a war short as a thunder shower—only wanted to re-establish the prewar order.[44]

Zechlin's interpretation neglects several important factors. For one thing, objectives of the September program like Mittelafrika and the annexation of Luxemburg go far beyond specific strategies for such a war. Also, Zechlin overlooks the fact that the prewar conception of Mitteleuropa included England in an economic constellation that was to rival North America and Russia. But the actual course of the war forced a change in this concept, and the Mitteleuropa plan was revised to be used against England. England was to be cut off from the French market and France "reserved" for German industry. This was not just a war measure, as the September program clearly states. The union was designed as a permanent arrangement to guarantee Germany economic, military, and political ascendancy in Europe.[45] German leaders agreed on this goal at the beginning of August 1914, four weeks before the September program (Zechlin's "war means") was drafted.[46] Later, Bethmann Hollweg himself often described this goal as a revision of the European balance of power. By broadening Germany's military, industrial, and agricultural base, it could, of course, serve strategic ends either in this war or in another. After the defeats on the Marne and at Ypres, the prospect of a second war became likely and was discussed with increasing frequency. Conceived in these terms, every peace is a means of war, and the September program, too, was a "means of war." But it was not merely a technical or tactical expedient to overcome an acute military crisis. It

44. B. von Bülow, *Denkwürdigkeiten*, vol. III, p. 148.
45. For the text of the September memorandum, see F. Fischer, *Griff nach der Weltmacht*, pp. 116 ff.
46. See the dissertation of J. Pragal.

was an expression of German striving for European hegemony, the first step toward "world domination" as envisaged by its prophets, Hans Delbrück and Kurt Riezler. The assumption behind the plan had always been a peace based on German victory. After the defeat of France and her incorporation into the German sphere of power, after the permanent weakening of Russia and her expulsion from eastern Europe, after the organization of a Mitteleuropa extending into the Balkans and the Orient, after the consolidation of Mittelafrika and northern Europe, England would have only two choices. She could either acknowledge this power constellation and submit to it, or she could embark on a second war for hegemony. In this second war, America might well support her if, as Rathenau warned, Germany forced her to seek American aid.[47]

47. F. Fischer, *Historische Zeitschrift,* 199/2, pp. 322 ff.

Not a Succession of Crises but the Persisting Desire for Power

The September program was subject to some change during its history: commitment to it fluctuated, specific points were modified, and the course of the war dictated shifts in emphasis between east and west. But the objectives originally stated in the program remained central in the political calculations of the German government and in the thinking of dominant social classes and political groups until the summer of 1918. The program summarized the guarantees and safeguards that were to make Germany's position in Europe unassailable and to establish her new place in the world.[1]

Mitteleuropa[2] was the main goal that Bethmann Hollweg, Kühlmann, and like-minded representatives of the chemical and electrical industries as well as of banks, big business, and shipping wanted to achieve. Spokesmen for the military and for heavy industry favored outright annexation. Zechlin's claim that the Mitteleuropa plan was abandoned on September 19, 1914, and that this decision was

---

1. For this whole problem, see F. Fischer, *Griff nach der Weltmacht.*
2. *Ibid.,* especially pp. 113 ff., 196 ff., 246 ff., 310 ff., 447 ff.

officially confirmed on October 22, 1914, mistakes technical questions about the application of customs policy for
the substance of the plan. Zechlin completely ignores the
fact that France was not defeated in October and November 1914 and therefore could not be included in a plan for
a German Mitteleuropa at that time. He does not think it
worth mentioning that Bethmann Hollweg never gave up
the basic idea of the customs union or, more important, of
Mitteleuropa as the organizational vehicle for establishing
German power in central Europe. The fact is that Mitteleuropa, possibly in the form of a customs union, remained
under discussion as an element of German war aims policy.
Contrary to Zechlin's presentation, the pertinent departments of Germany and Prussia met in November 1914 and
throughout that winter to discuss all possible consequences
of the chancellor's Mitteleuropa plan.[3] Only at this time
did the upper levels of the bureaucracy begin to "focus" on
the project. It was obvious that differences would emerge
and specific modifications be sought, especially by Prussia.
But despite all objections from the departments, the project
remained unchanged as a "guideline." This was true even
when apparent reorientations of German policy took place.
Discussions of Mitteleuropa were temporarily suspended in
the spring and summer of 1915 because of attempts to conclude a separate peace with Russia.[4] Bethmann Hollweg believed a Mitteleuropa with high tariffs would discriminate
against Russian exports and interfere with his peace efforts.
But when these attempts failed in the autumn of 1915,[5] the
Mitteleuropa project was taken up again and the main emphasis placed on close commercial and military ties with
Austria-Hungary. Its implementation was the subject of nu-

3. See the summary on numerous conferences in the appendix to Delbrück's memorandum to Bethmann Hollweg, April 12, 1915, in
Deutsches Zentralarchiv, Potsdam, RK, Mitteleuropäischer Wirt-
schaftsbund, vol. 2, no. 404; see also DZA Potsdam, AA, HA, Öster-
reich 580, vol. 1, no. 3986, memorandum of Müller, October 25,
1914.
4. F. Fischer, *Griff nach der Weltmacht,* pp. 229 ff.
5. *Ibid.,* pp. 242 ff.

merous conferences until the summer of 1918. To prepare
the way for it, the government drew on all existing and
newly created economic unions, and utilized propaganda
like Friedrich Naumann's book.[6] The demise of the Mitteleuropa plan was not the result of a German policy decision. The Polish question, which had become acute after
the occupation of Poland in 1915, divided Germany and
Austria-Hungary over the issue of Mitteleuropa. As early as
September 1914 Bethmann Hollweg had included Poland
in his plans for Mitteleuropa. Now, within the framework
of the economic reorganization of Europe, Poland was to
be drawn into greater "dependency" on Germany or, more
specifically, on Prussia. But Austria-Hungary had similar
goals. By linking the "Polish solution" to Mitteleuropa,
Germany found an alternative to her policy of indirect
domination. The alternative, which she adopted in 1918,
was direct domination of both Austria-Hungary and Poland. Vienna's political involvement in determining what
shape Poland's future government should take put a strain
on the Habsburg monarchy and so impaired its military
strength that Austria-Hungary itself increasingly became an
object of German war aims. Here again we see prewar policy remaining in force.[7] Mitteleuropa, which continued to
include Belgium as well as Poland (and which was to include France if she could be forced to join), remained such
a constant war aim that the fall of Bethmann Hollweg in no
way affected it. On the contrary, the negotiations between
Czernin and Kühlmann in October 1917, though changing
the emphasis of the policy, made it more ambitious in
scope. Although the framework of a Mitteleuropa remained, the organization of the bloc was to be determined
strictly by German interests.[8] Now Germany not only tried

6. F. Naumann, *Mitteleuropa* (Berlin, 1915).
7. See the dissertation of my student D. Löding.
8. Österreichisches Staatsarchiv, HHStA, PA, I, XLVII/13, red carton
   524, guidelines of October 22, 1917.

"to subjugate" Austria-Hungary and Poland but also laid claim to Rumania, the "million-mark prize." As late as August 1918, Chancellor Hertling asserted that the achievement of such a union, based on a firm alliance with the Austro-Hungarian monarchy, would *create a central European bloc of a strength never before experienced in the history of the world.*" [9]

The *plan to weaken Russia* or to create "safeguards" against her also remained constant.[10] Not only the Pan-Germans—or, to use Ritter's terminology, the "German patriots" (with their annexationist desires)—but also the German leaders themselves developed ambitious plans for security in the east. After military defeat in the west in November 1914, the scope of these plans was reduced in the hope of concluding a separate peace with Russia. The so-called Polish border strip now became Germany's main objective.[11] Its "preparation" was assigned to Wahnschaffe of the Chancellery. Hindenburg presented the basic military demands in the form of a map, which disappeared from the files after their return to the Federal Republic of Germany.[12] Later, Ludendorff could point to these demands and justifiably describe this eastern policy as Bethmann Hollweg's. After 1916, a policy of "liberation and of creating buffer states"—described euphemistically today as a "policy of separation" [13]—guided German planning. Bethmann Hollweg unequivocally advocated this policy when he declared on April 5, 1916, that "the peoples between the

9. Deutsches Zentralarchiv, Potsdam, RK Krieg 18, no. 2458/4, Hertling to Wilhelm II, August 15, 1918. My italics.
10. F. Fischer, *Griff nach der Weltmacht,* pp. 128 ff., 155 ff., 257 ff., 346 ff., 561 ff., 627 ff., 714 ff.
11. Cf. the dissertation of my student I. Geiss, published as *Der polnische Grenzstreifen 1914–1918* (Lübeck and Hamburg), 1960.
12. Deutsches Zentralarchiv, Potsdam, RK, Krieg 15, vol. 1, no. 2442/10, Hindenburg to Bethmann Hollweg and Bethmann Hollweg's answer, December 13, 1914.
13. See the work of Rothfels' student B. Mann, *Die baltischen Länder in der deutschen Kriegszielpublizistik,* Tübinger Studien zur Geschichte und Politik, vol. 19 (Tübingen, 1965).

Baltic Sea and the Volhynian swamps, be they Poles, Lithuanians, Balts, or Letts, whom Germany and her allies had
liberated will never be voluntarily abandoned to the reactionary regime of Russia." [14]

This policy, formulated by the chancellor before his fall
in the spring of 1917,[15] was realized in the peace treaties of
Brest Litovsk and Bucharest. These treaties—consigned to
oblivion by Germans and German historians—imposed a
new political orientation on Poland, Lithuania, Courland,
the Ukraine, the northern Baltic area, Finland, Georgia,
and Transcaucasia. Russia's military setbacks and the Revolution, promoted by Germany, enabled Germany to realize her goals.[16]

At times, this "security policy" overshadowed the Mitteleuropa concept. The "border states policy" won increasing
support as military success in the east allowed the Germans
to use not only international law but statute law as well to
transform border states "separated" from Russia into German vassal states with German dynasties. The hope of making Rump Russia—Lenin's Russia of 1918—at least economically dependent on Germany was also a central motive
in this eastern policy. This aim became eminently clear in
extensive plans German industrialists made in the summer
of 1918 for opening Russia to German trade.[17]

Brest Litovsk reflected not the mentality of Ludendorff
and the High Command alone but the mentality of Germany as a whole. It found the enthusiastic support and
praise of all elements "loyal to the state," including the
churches and the political parties (except for the Majority

14. F. Fischer, *Griff nach der Weltmacht*, p. 297.
15. Deutsches Zentralarchiv, Potsdam, RK, Grosses Hauptquartier 21,
     Beiheft, Handakten, Kriegsziele, no. 2477, March 27, 1917.
16. F. Fischer, *Griff nach der Weltmacht*, pp. 450 ff.
17. Deutsches Zentralarchiv, Potsdam, Spezialbüro Helfferich, no.
     19285, Protokoll, May 16, 1918, and Spezialbüro Helfferich, Russ-
     land, Friedensverhandlungen, Allgemeine, no. 19285, Report of a
     meeting in RWA, June 4, 1918; Auswärtiges Amt Bonn, Deutsch-
     land 131, vol. 45, Erzberger to Joffe.

Socialists, who abstained, and the Independent Socialists, who opposed).[18]

The *plan for Belgium* [19] was probably the most constant element in German war aims policy throughout the war. Since adherence to the plan cannot be denied, Ritter and Zechlin typically speak of a "most fateful continuity"; and in their approach to this matter, history gives way to metaphysics. In fact, there were persisting demands for the annexation of Liège and the territory east of the Maas. As late as 1918, the military still considered the Maas line essential. Also, the navy had designs on the Flemish coast, on Antwerp, and on the harbor triangle of Brugge-Seebrugge-Ostende (probably on the French canal ports of Calais, Boulogne, and Dunkirk as well). But even if we disregard these extreme demands, Germany's basic objective in Belgium—often negatively expressed—remained the same: Belgium was to be "penetrated" economically, militarily, and politically, and made a tributary or vassal state. One component in this policy of "penetration" was a plan to support the Flemish minority and to divide Belgium into two states or administrative areas. Belgium was never again to serve as an enemy glacis. These aspirations are reflected in efforts to conclude a separate peace with Belgium in 1915 and 1916.[20]

The offensives in the spring and summer of 1918 were expected to produce a military situation on the western front that would enable Germany to conclude peace on her own terms. The German departments and the office of the Governor-General carried on extensive preliminary discussions about these terms, and my work on German war aims has far from exhausted this material. The plans for Belgium most fully reveal the harsh consistency of Germany's aims to increase and secure power. These were not strategies, not

18. F. Fischer, *Griff nach der Weltmacht,* pp. 668 ff.
19. *Ibid.,* pp. 268 ff., 327 ff., 363 ff., 583 ff., 801 ff.
20. *Ibid.,* pp. 268 ff.

means of war, as Zechlin would have it, but goals to be achieved by war.

Plans for Luxemburg and Longwy-Briey also remained unchanged. Policy for Luxemburg, a member of the German customs union at the time, was permanently·established in the curt formulation of the September program: "Luxemburg will become a German federal state." [21] As late as October 1918, Hindenburg demanded the annexation of Luxemburg. Zechlin makes much of the fact that the border area of Longwy-Briey, which Germany occupied in August 1914, was taken into the protective custody of the state and that property owners were not legally dispossessed. But the explanation for these measures cannot be found in the idea of a "limited war" or in moral considerations.[22] The German documents clearly indicate that internal German disagreements delayed annexation. German leaders had not yet agreed on what should be done with the Longwy-Briey ore deposits after France had ceded the territory by peace treaty. The deposits could be transferred either to private industry or—in accordance with the principles of so-called war socialism—to state ownership on the model of the Prussian state mines. But there was never any doubt among German leaders that France would lose Longwy-Briey. As innumerable studies on the question indicate,[23] civil and military leaders realized completely what this change of ownership would mean for both countries.

Mittelafrika [24] also remained a constant goal of Ger-

21. Deutsches Zentralarchiv, Potsdam, RK, Grosses Hauptquartier 21, no. 2476, Bethmann Hollweg to Delbrück, September 9, 1914.
22. E. Zechlin, *Historische Zeitschrift,* 199/2, pp. 366 ff.
23. See the following files in Deutsches Zentralarchiv, Potsdam: RdI 5, Erzgebiet von Longwy-Briey, vol. I, no. 19305; RWA Wirtschaftliche Verhandlungen in den besetzten Gebieten, 2, Frankreich, no. 876/1; RWA Friedensverhandlungen mit Frankreich, March 1915 to November 1918, no. 1883 and Brieybecken, no. 1884; RWA, Besetzte Gebiete 2, Frankreich Erze, no. 877.
24. F. Fischer, *Griff nach der Weltmacht,* especially pp. 469 ff. and 791 ff.

many's expansionist desires throughout the war, and her plan for it shows only a few modifications, all of which broadened the scope of the project. We can easily establish a continuity in this aim from the preliminary stages of Anglo-German negotiations in 1912–14 onward, even in terms of personnel. Solf and Kühlmann were its two main advocates both before and during the war. During the war, Solf considered the plan "academic" because of the geographical remoteness of central Africa, but he gradually came to see the project as a substitute goal, diverting national attention from "absurd" demands for annexation in Europe. The nation and its leadership, however, had always seen central Africa, with the copper mines of Katanga its single most valuable asset, as a complement to the economic community envisaged in the Mitteleuropa plan. Naval demands for bases on the islands off the African coast were added to the Mittelafrika plan.

Plans for the Balkans, the Near East, Transcaucasia, and a "thrust" toward India [25] also go back to prewar policy and were consistently pursued during the entire war. To be sure, the alliance with the Ottoman Empire led Germany to adopt a more indirect method of domination than she had planned before the war. This indirect domination took the form of requiring extensive mining and other rights in Turkey as security for massive war loans. The Germans thus began to crowd out prewar English, French, and Belgian competition. As Turkey's military power declined, she, like Germany's older ally Austria-Hungary, increasingly became an object of the German desire for power.

Efforts to separate Transcaucasia from Bolshevik Russia and to establish a German vassal state in Georgia also reveal the continuity of German war aims before and during the war. Germany spent millions on propaganda before the

25. *Ibid.*, pp. 146 ff., 402 ff., 466 ff., 684 ff., and 738 ff.

war and constantly encouraged insurrections during the war, with the ultimate objective of creating a land bridge to central Asia as a "threat to the English position in India." [26] The pursuit of this goal casts two points about German policy into bold relief. One is that the German government and German industry shared the same basic objectives. The exploitation of rich manganese, chromium, and oil deposits in the Caucasus and in Transcaucasia was primarily a war aim, not just a matter of strategic importance. But here, as in the Ukraine, Germany sacrificed a strategic advantage in her attempt to achieve a long-term objective. The other point is that Germany, in her quest for power, did not hesitate to disregard her Turkish ally's plans for the annexation of Transcaucasia.

The consistent pursuit of German political, economic, and military goals during the war—goals formulated for the most part before the war—attest to the strength of Germany's desire for world power. Seen from this perspective, the thesis that "Kühlmann continued along Bethmann Hollweg's path" is valid. At the late date of 1964, only German historians still take the language of the German government of 1914–18 at face value, and only German historians still claim that the ultimate goal of German policy during the First World War was to achieve a compromise peace. In his review of Wolfgang Steglich's book *Die Friedenspolitik der Mittelmächte 1917–1918* (*The Peace Policy of the Central Powers 1917–1918*), volume I, 1964, Zechlin [27] expresses his agreement with Steglich and asserts, contrary to my interpretation of German policy in World War I as a "policy of war aims," that Germany's intent was of "precisely the opposite nature," that is, a "policy of peace." Zechlin states that the "guiding principles of German policy" were not the

26. Auswärtiges Amt Bonn, Russland 97a, Grünau to the Foreign Ministry, June 7, 1918.
27. *Die Zeit,* no. 10, 1965, p. 10.

"war aims extensively discussed" by me but "strivings for security and, later in the war, for the survival of Germany." Steglich in no way denies the existence of war aims, Zechlin goes on to say, but he correctly sees them as "aspects of Germany's desire for security. These aims were not rigidly fixed, and—this is the crucial point—they remained permanently subordinate" to the desire for security. Thus, Steglich finds precisely those political tendencies in Kühlmann's thinking that Zechlin claims to have found in Bethmann Hollweg's during the first months of war.

My critics' blind acceptance of Bethmann Hollweg's "security" slogan and their emphatic declaration that German war aims fluctuated with what seemed feasible at any given stage of the war supposedly prove the existence of a German "peace policy" and show how unjustifiable it is to speak of a war aims policy. The peace of Brest Litovsk demonstrated what "seemed feasible," and the meaning of the German nation's "desire for security" became eminently clear in that agreement. But Steglich and Zechlin fail to see this meaning. The treaty does not reflect German willingness to conclude a separate peace after defeat on the western front in November 1914—a willingness that my critics call the decisive factor of German war aims policy. Instead, it reflects what Germany's war aims had been all along. Despite changing conditions, Germany held firmly to the goal of extending her power. Even after the failure of the original war plan and the sacrifice of hundreds of thousands of men in an all-out gamble, Germany—though she did limit her goals for a short time—continued undeterred in her policy of securing world power. This policy had nothing to do with the "survival" of Germany within the framework of the *status quo*.

Germany's war aims—varying in form and scope but unchanging in objectives—also reveal a unity of state and society, of politics and economics, that first developed during the war and that could have developed to such a degree only at that time. This unity shows, too, that German war aims and the effort to achieve them had nothing to do with reaction to outside pressures but originated in Germany's commitment to a decisive struggle that would either raise her to world leadership or plunge her into utter defeat.

The Pursuit of World Power: Commitment, Not Reaction

The expansion of German power, which the government termed "securing" the Reich and which the leading classes of the nation demanded and sanctioned, was in no way a reaction to enemy claims. It originated in Germany alone and was rooted in prewar assumptions and aspirations.

As early as 1903 the Bismarck specialist Erich Marcks said in a lecture on the "imperialistic idea in today's world":

Foreigners complain that Germany, more methodically than other nations, is imposing herself on the world through colonial acquisitions, through expansion of her economic influence, through shipping lines, railroad construction, capital loans, through temporal and ecclesiastical agencies, through the establishment and strengthening of ties with ethnically related groups, through protectionism and military build-up, and through annexation by force—in short, through all the means of the new system. They accuse us, the latecomers, of having disturbed the peaceful tranquility and the old balance of power by our entry into the competitive arena. This criticism does not disturb us. . . . We are in the midst of a world development which some deplore but which we must accept and take an active part in if we are not to be completely crushed and excluded from the ranks of the world's vital nations.[1]

Thus, Marcks approved of annexation by force as a means and goal of German policy. The "old liberalism" was dead:

The idea of increased state autonomy, the idea of power, has replaced it. It is this idea that inspires and guides leading men everywhere. Quite apart from Russia, where this spirit has never disappeared, we find this same motivating force in Roosevelt and Chamberlain, as well as in Bismarck and Kaiser Wilhelm II.[2]

Marcks formulated these thoughts shortly after 1900. During the following years they kept recurring with few variations at all important levels of society, and they were carried over into the war. Annexations and overseas acquisitions were to serve the goal of extending Germany's influence in the world.

It is generally accepted that Wilhelm II's "world policy" of 1897–98 encouraged the acquisition of new overseas possessions, colonies, or spheres of influence; but it is generally forgotten that the idea of strengthening Germany's position in Europe was a corollary of this "world policy." The idea did not first emerge from the disappointment and bitterness felt in 1911, when the rejection of German demands by France and England precipitated a build-up of the German army as well as of the navy. In a lecture to the local chapter of the Naval League on January 25, 1912, the Heidelberg historian Hermann Oncken argued for

1. E. Marcks, *Männer und Zeiten*, vol. II (Leipzig, 1911), p. 287.
2. *Ibid.*, p. 290.

"weakening our opponent [England] in the world arena where he poses the greatest threat to us—in his system of continental alliances." [3]

Even before 1900, spokesmen for the Pan-German Association (*Alldeutscher Verband*) demanded the creation of a central European customs union. In his work *Deutsche Weltpolitik* (*German World Policy*), Professor Hasse of Leipzig proclaimed such a customs union as the great task for the present generation.[4] In the same year, he had spoken to the Reichstag about "a central European customs union that must inevitably come." This organization would bring together in an economic union the areas which were once included in the old German Reich—Germany, Austria-Hungary, Belgium, Holland, and Switzerland, with Rumania as the bridge to the East. Such a grouping would create the most advantageous economic bloc conceivable. These ideas, amplified to include France, were taken up in 1912–14 by Bernhardi and Walter Rathenau, among others; and these men influenced the Kaiser and leading policy-makers in turn.

It is unjustified to give undue emphasis to the mood on the "threshold of war" and to claim that it accounts for a drastic change in Germany's perception of her place in the world.

On the contrary, Germany had thought war inevitable for some time; and only war offered hope that an expansion of German power would be achieved—war, "the moving force of mankind" (Schmoller, writing in the Vienna *Neue Freie Presse* on March 23, 1913),[5] war, which has always "proved to be the great cause of spiritual rejuvenation in the state, society, economy, and in all aspects of culture"

3. H. Oncken, *Historisch-Politische Aufsätze und Reden* (Munich and Berlin, 1914), p. 187.
4. Cf. A. Kruck, *Geschichte des Alldeutschen Verbandes* (Wiesbaden, 1954), p. 43.
5. Quoted from Schmoller, *Zwanzig Jahre deutscher Politik* (Munich and Leipzig, 1920), p. 120.

(Erich Marcks, 1903).[6] After the disappointing outcome of the second Moroccan crisis, Admiral Valois consoled his readers with a brochure which the conservative *Kreuzzeitung* reprinted with favorable comments on May 8, 1912:

Some proponents of colonial acquisition may not be satisfied with what was achieved, but let them rest assured that the division of continental possessions among the European powers will not be accomplished by claims on territory and colonial treaties. These decisions will be made only on the great European battlefields of the future.[7]

The statements of the Chief of General Staff, von Moltke, lend these remarks greater significance. Moltke expressed regret after 1909 that Germany had not waged a preventive war. When the Austro-Hungarian Chief of General Staff, Conrad, conveyed to Moltke in May 1913 his "regrets that the Balkan question is apparently to be resolved by diplomatic means,"[8] Moltke answered on May 20, 1913, through the Austro-Hungarian military attaché in Berlin, Bienerth. Bienerth reported as follows: "Concerning the purely diplomatic solution of the Scutari question, His Excellency [Moltke] agrees completely with Your Excellency's view. This is only a postponement, not a solution. Consequently, steps are being taken to strengthen the Germany army."[9]

As Bethmann Hollweg's letter of February 10, 1913, shows, German diplomacy held back in view of the fact that English neutrality was not assured. These delaying tactics disappointed Moltke, and the military resigned itself to await the consequences of expanding the armed forces.

6. E. Marcks, *Männer und Zeiten,* vol. II, p. 291.
7. *Kreuzzeitung,* no. 115.
8. Conrad, vol. III, p. 317.
9. *Ibid.,* p. 328.

In October 1913, the Kaiser assured Conrad of German support in a third Balkan war.[10] This conflict was to become the First World War. Moltke was convinced of the imminence of a major war; and on the same day, when he became aware of differences between Conrad and Francis Ferdinand, who was reluctant to go to war, Moltke urged Conrad not to resign: "Don't quit. Now that we're on the verge of war, you must remain." [11] A few days later, at the beginning of November 1913, the Kaiser and Moltke repeated their predictions of war in their well-known Berlin conference with King Albert of Belgium.

When the great war broke out in August 1914, the hour of "reckoning" with France and Russia had come. Germany hoped to leave both these powers permanently weakened after their military defeat and thus to "secure" Germany's position in Europe. This goal was to be achieved in part through direct annexation of strategically or economically important areas, in part through indirect affiliation of buffer states ("defiliation," from the point of view of the states involved) or through treaties that would put Germany in the forefront of nations.

When the outcome of the Marne battle became known (everywhere but in Germany), reports of Germany's desire for peace appeared in the Entente press. The German government answered with an announcement in the semi-official *Norddeutsche Allgemeine Zeitung* of September 16, 1914: "In reply to this falsification, we declare that the German people will not lay down their weapons in this struggle, which was viciously forced upon them, until they have won the *security* necessary for their *future* in the world." [12]

This was a public use of the terms Bethmann Hollweg had recently formulated in policy discussions when he out-

10. *Ibid.*, p. 470.
11. *Ibid.*
12. *Völkerkrieg*, no. 1, p. 321.

lined German demands after victory. In his introduction to the September program, his phrase had been "securing Germany's position in the east and west for all time." [13] A week before the announcement in the *Norddeutsche Allgemeine Zeitung,* when victory still seemed likely, Bethmann Hollweg had sent the September program to Berlin to establish tentative guidelines for the conclusion of peace with France.

In mid-November 1914, it became clear that the original war plan had failed, and Bethmann Hollweg found it necessary to bolster the nation's morale. In a speech to the Reichstag on December 2, a speech that differed from his previous one on August 4 because of its anti-English bias, he expressed German war aims in the following terms:

. . . let us unite in a solemn vow to persevere to the last breath so that our children and grandchildren can continue to augment the greatness of the Reich in a stronger Germany that is free and *secure* from outside threats and force . . . we shall hold on until we have the certainty that no one will ever dare disturb our peace again. . . . [14]

An article in the *Temps* of September 9, 1914, claimed that the German government had suggested the idea of mediation to the President of the United States; but on October 16, 1914, the *Kölnische Zeitung* asserted in a semi-official response that the German government wanted "to make absolutely clear that the German people, who had sacrificed so much, can accept only a peace that provides them with guarantees for their *security* in the future and protects them against new attacks." [15]

For five months, war had been waged along very definite

13. The September program is quoted from Fischer, *Griff nach der Weltmacht,* p. 116.
14. *Völkerkrieg,* no. 3, p. 11.
15. *Ibid.,* p. 17.

guidelines and with very detailed plans for a peace based on victory. But no reference had been made to the war aims of the Entente. The only dangers mentioned were the alleged threat to Germany that the very existence of the neighboring states always constituted, even in peacetime, and the "attack" which was read into the July crisis. (After all, the Germans were not nihilists and were consistent enough to adhere to the assumptions and values they had built up over many years, even when they chose to carry on politics by other means.)

In the summer of 1915, the advance on the eastern front restored the confidence of the Central Powers; and when the American news agency United Press inquired on August 5 what conditions "Germany considered essential to insure peace in Europe and to promote European civilization effectively," [16] the German government's reply of August 9 took the success of the Central Powers into account and declared, as the Kaiser had in all his statements, that Germany "is fighting for a peace which will give Germany and the powers fighting on Germany's side the permanent *security* necessary for their national *future*." [17]

For the Americans, whom the sinking of the *Lusitania* had alienated, the additional point was made that a German victory would put an end to England's naval predominance and insure freedom of the seas to all nations, including the United States.

The chancellor indicated in his speech to the Reichstag on December 9, 1915, that securing Germany's future would alter the face of Europe.[18] Carefully seeking a middle line between the moderates and the radicals of the Right, he stated explicitly that the present balance of power in Europe would have to come to an end. Bethmann Holl-

---

16. *Völkerkrieg,* no. 7, p. 5.
17. *Ibid.,* p. 6.
18. F. Thimme, *Bethmann Hollwegs Kriegsreden* (Stuttgart and Berlin, 1919), p. 87. See too, F. Fischer, *Griff nach der Weltmacht,* pp. 264 f.

weg repeated this demand on April 5, 1916, when he declared that the Poles, Lithuanians, Balts, and Letts, who had been freed by Germany and her allies, could never again be returned to foreign domination.[19]

Invoking the principle of national self-determination, the German Foreign Ministry created the so-called League of the Foreign Peoples of Russia. The main purpose of this was to make a favorable impression on public opinion in the United States and in other countries.[20] The League's task was to coordinate the propaganda activities of the various individual national committees, which were already more or less dependent on Germany, and to win them for a public proclamation. This, too, was an expression of Germany's commitment to power, not a reaction to outside pressures.

In April 1916, when victory in the battle of Verdun still seemed likely, Ernst Bassermann, the leader of the National Liberal Party, published an article entitled "Power." [21] According to the semi-official war chronicle *Der Völkerkrieg*, Bassermann's article "reflects the views held by most of the German people." [22] Bassermann asserted that in the prewar period the imperialism of the nineteenth century had become more pronounced and had prepared the way for war:

In the course of this development in the twentieth century, power has emerged as the dominant factor everywhere. [For Germany, too, ascendancy in the world has become a basic problem, and war aims policy has to be considered from this point of view.] When the time comes to lay down our weapons, future policy will be based on the maxim: "After victory, take the sword more firmly in hand." Only a position of great power will allow us to cultivate the works of peace. Let others hate us because of our power as long as they fear us! Power! The twentieth century will continue to stand under the aegis of this magic

19. F. Fischer, *Griff nach der Weltmacht*, p. 297.
20. *Ibid.*, pp. 172 f. and 296.
21. *Völkerkrieg*, no. 16 (1917), pp. 1 ff.
22. *Ibid.*, p. 1.

word. Power is the sole prerequisite and basis for the existence of even such populous nations as Germany.[23]

He was even clearer in regard to war aims:

We cannot return to the *status quo ante*. Frederick the Great recognized this when he said: "Any war that does not produce conquests weakens the victor and enervates the state." [24]

Again, there is no mention of Entente war aims. An article in the *Kölnische Zeitung* of September 12, 1916, shows how little the war aims of the Triple Entente affected German thinking. The article examined Russian war aims and concluded that the Russian war effort, "to the extent that it is aggressive at all anymore," was directed to the south. But even the old Russian dream of taking Constantinople had been shattered by German victories in Rumania. Because of Russia's weakness, Germany saw no reason to limit her goals:

We had already achieved our war aims in the east by mid-1916. . . . Panslavic desires for conquests have long since been eradicated at their source in the northwest Balkans, and the area has been put under sound German administration. The ambitions of Greater Russia in the north have been thwarted, and the strategic railroad system is in the hands of the victors. The Panslavic movement has been turned back to the east. The University of Warsaw and the promised gift of freedom for Poland are the first rewards to be realized from this completed cultural mission.[25]

In the west, England was to lose her hegemony:

We have already won freedom of the seas. The idea of one state dominating the world is a thing of the past. Decadent as a

23. *Ibid.*, p. 2.
24. *Ibid.*, p. 3.
25. *Völkerkrieg*, no. 20, p. 1.

state, nation, and society, England is sinking even now from her leading position in the world to that of just another power among six or seven others. . . . These are Germany's war aims in the east and in the west. It is appropriate to direct attention to them and to discuss them.[26]

Diverting attention away from the limited goals of annexation in the east and west, the writer turned toward "distant" realms where he thought Germany's future lay. In this, he was closer to Bethmann Hollweg than to the military.

The aims for eastern Europe, programmatically stated here, were realized in the peace of Brest Litovsk. German aims in the west were to be achieved by a great, final effort in the spring of 1918. The struggle to the death between Slavs and Germans, so often conjured up before the war by Kaiser Wilhelm II, Moltke, Stumm, Jagow, Bethmann Hollweg, and others, had, it seemed, been decided conclusively in favor of the Germans. It remained to be shown to the English, who were traitors from the racial point of view, "that German might had defended England's interests as well." [27]

As I have shown, political, economic, and intellectual forces at work in the nation contributed to the determination to make Germany "secure." Erdmann comes to quite different conclusions in his interpretation, based exclusively on Bethmann Hollweg's statements. Erdmann writes:

It is significant that Bethmann Hollweg's statements about enhancing Germany's position occur in Riezler's diary for the first time only during the war, not before it and not during the July crisis of 1914. They are a product of the war, not a cause of it. Defense is their primary concern. To prevent east and west from joining forces against her with any prospect of success in

26. *Ibid.,* p. 2.
27. *Ibid.,* p. 1.

the future, Germany found it desirable to extend her political, economic and military security beyond her own borders.[28]

It is possible that the Bethmann Hollweg of the Riezler diary (i.e., not the Chancellor Bethmann Hollweg whose views are documented in countless other sources) did not voice these ideas until the war. But as I have shown above, these ideas had been often and emphatically stated before the war. Riezler himself is a case in point. In his book *Grundzüge der Weltpolitik* (*Fundamentals of World Politics*), published under the pseudonym Ruedorffer, he asserted that the German position on the continent must become so strong in the future that no conceivable coalition could impose its will on Germany.[29] Here again, this illustrates a desire for power, not a reaction to outside forces.

But more important than these aspects of Erdmann's statement is the fact that a German historian in 1964 could still uncritically accept the thesis that Germany was attacked. My book *Krieg der Illusionen* (*War of Illusions*) demonstrates that the German government formulated this thesis at the end of the July crisis. Germany did this to shift responsibility for the war to the enemy powers and so to justify its own war aims. Since these aims were expansionist by any objective standard, the German government resorted to the fiction of an attack to make them seem "defensive." Erdmann completely overlooks the point that these "security measures" had to be given a defensive cast for the benefit of those Germans who would only support a war of defense and also for the benefit of neutral countries like the United States (1914–15).

Having rescued Bethmann Hollweg's soul, or image, Erdmann can then grant that the sum total of these security

28. K. D. Erdmann, *Geschichte in Wissenschaft und Unterricht*, 15, Heft 9 (1964), p. 539.
29. K. Riezler, *Grundzüge der Weltpolitik*, pp. 106 f.

measures meant German hegemony in Europe, which in turn was to have served as a basis for world supremacy. By introducing the exaggerated term "world domination," which I never used, Erdmann tries to cast a more favorable light on Bethmann Hollweg's involvement in the pursuit of world power. Erdmann shows us a tragic Bethmann Hollweg "who controlled power without being addicted to power." [30] The term "world domination" comes, incidentally, from the arsenal of the philosopher Kurt Riezler, who attributed to all major nations the innate tendency to achieve that goal.[31]

The older man may well have reacted with caution to the younger Riezler's concept of world domination, but such ideas were widespread nonetheless. Hans Delbrück, professor at the University of Berlin and editor of the *Preussische Jahrbücher,* could say in 1912:

It was true in the past that our fleet was created to protect our commerce. But today we can set ourselves a higher goal. The purpose of our fleet is not only to protect our overseas trade but also to bring us our fair share of that world domination which is allotted to civilized nations by the very nature of mankind and its higher destiny.[32]

And Delbrück continues in a more metaphysical vein:

. . . The earth is given to men . . . for the sake of the true and ultimate good, the nation . . . not to conduct business upon but to dominate.[33]

It is worth noting that even an interpretation like Erdmann's, bent on apologia and on honoring its hero (in this

---

30. K. D. Erdmann, *Geschichte in Wissenschaft und Unterricht,* 15, Heft 9 (1964), p. 540.
31. K. Riezler, *Grundzüge der Weltpolitik,* pp. 31 ff.
32. *Preussische Jahrbücher,* vol. 149 (1912), p. 365.
33. *Ibid.,* p. 363.

case a hero of peace), must grant that "such a build-up of German power in Europe—though in the form of dominating neighboring states rather than incorporating foreign territory—amounted to a campaign for hegemony in central Europe"; and this in turn served as the point of departure for "becoming a world power." [34]

If this was indeed Germany's policy—and all the documents support this view—then the question of whether or not Bethmann Hollweg himself may have felt uncomfortable about it is of no importance whatsoever. The crucial point is that the Germany he represented pursued this policy.

Erdmann's efforts at apologia outdo themselves in the unintentionally comic assertion that the September program "is in no way an expression of confidence in victory." [35] Even if Bethmann Hollweg had had only very limited intelligence, he must have realized that the fulfillment of the September program was dependent on total victory. He did, of course, realize this, and he always dealt with the question of war aims with the expectation of victory in mind. And victory meant the fulfillment of demands, even for Bethmann Hollweg. But his desires are not as significant as the will of the nation.

34. K. D. Erdmann, *Geschichte in Wissenschaft und Unterricht,* 15, Heft 9 (1964), p. 539.
35. *Ibid.,* p. 538.

Not Bethmann Hollweg's Aims but Germany's Aims

The demands of the economy as well as the ideas and hopes of the intellectual elite determined prewar policy, and policy during the war must be judged in terms of these forces, too. German war aims policy cannot be reduced to the political calculations and aspirations of a single person, even if that person is the chancellor. Ritter discounts the war aims formulated in innumerable memoranda and petitions as the pipe dreams of irresponsible power-worshippers. Zechlin describes them as the inconsequential proposals of tiresome "meddlers." Even with a state as conservative and bureaucratic as the German Reich, the historian must take the power of pressure groups into account. Neither Ritter's nor Zechlin's approach does so. The overwhelming mass of evidence demonstrating Germany's will to power and her sense of mission makes it untenable to confine the examination of German war aims policy to the narrow area of biographical analysis.

To be sure, the psychological analysis of important individuals has been and still is the most popular field of German historiography. Consistent with this tradition, Erdmann has tried to present and judge the German government's policy exclusively from the point of view of Bethmann Hollweg's individual personality and inner conflict.[1] The particular origin of the Riezler diary raises problems in evaluating it as a historical document, but quite apart from these questions, we must still remember that the individual personality is only *one* factor the historian has to consider. Concentrating exclusively on psychological issues detracts from the study of concrete factors involved in pragmatic decisions. Important as the results of a "psychoanalysis" can be for the historian, history cannot be limited to this one type of study, which is all too frequently regarded as the "appropriate" task of German historiography.[2] Such limitation disregards social, economic, political, and intellectual forces.

Although Bethmann Hollweg alone was responsible to the Kaiser (not to the German people) for German policy, he was not Germany's only spokesman. The nation had other representatives: the political parties ranging from the Conservatives to the Center (These parties joined forces as the so-called war aims majority from August 1914 to July 1917 and again after November 1917); the exponents of economic power; the numerous political and economic associations; and, last but not least, the most influential groups of the nation's intellectual elite. Ritter describes the situation in this way: "As the Kaiser's right-hand man, the chancellor seemed independent of the parties and of public opinion. But in fact he was harassed and worried by them and forced from one makeshift solution and compromise to

---

1. K. D. Erdmann, *Geschichte in Wissenschaft und Unterricht,* 15, Heft 9 (1964).
2. G. Ritter, *Staatskunst und Kriegshandwerk,* vol. III, p. 613, note 71. Ritter criticizes me for not asking what he regards as the most important question, namely, "with what inner reservations . . . the Chancellor had all these studies prepared."

another." [3] This is an accurate description of the chancellor's position if one disregards the strongly emotional formulations of the second sentence. The influence of these groups became particularly clear after the outbreak of war, when they demanded periodic declarations from the government to the effect that if victory were won, safeguards and guarantees would be established to assure Germany an unassailable position among nations.

In a review of recent research in *Geschichte in Wissenschaft und Unterricht,*[4] Hans Herzfeld stresses that "to minimize the importance of the office Bethmann Hollweg held —an office with inherent strengths and weaknesses—would be to misunderstand the very nature of Wilhelminian Germany." I have always called attention to this "office" and to the conditions imposed on it by the German governmental system. At the same time, as Herzfeld quite correctly says, I have also reproached traditional German historiography for its "typical overemphasis of subjective and individual elements in Bethmann Hollweg's personality." Since it cannot be denied that the chancellor, Germany's highest official, was actively involved in war aims policy, Ritter has split Bethmann Hollweg into an "office" and a "personality" to rescue his hero's integrity. (In his discussion, Herzfeld is mistaken about the date of my essay in the *Historische Zeitschrift*. This essay could not be an answer to Ritter's *Staatskunst und Kriegshandwerk* [*The Sword and the Scepter*], volume III, which first appeared in late 1964.) I would like to state once more that the historically relevant factors were the very office Bethmann Hollweg held and the forces that both sustained it and defined its limits. A policy of compromise resulted from this situation. Subtle changes occur in Ritter's and Herzfeld's presentations of the chancellor's personality. From the end of World War I to the end of World War II, Bethmann Hollweg appeared in their ac-

3. *Ibid.,* p. 21.
4. H. Herzfeld, *Geschichte in Wissenschaft und Unterricht,* 16, Heft 7 (1965), pp. 455 ff.

counts as a great bungler who failed to make adequate military and diplomatic preparations for war and could not unify the nation behind the military effort. But after 1945 the weakness of the "philosopher of Hohenfinow" became his "strength"—and his tragedy. As both Ritter and Herzfeld emphasize, Bethmann Hollweg's policy "clearly" could not succeed, a policy which, despite its element of power politics, they now describe in positive terms as one of "moderation." [5]

After discussing the wording of his speech at length with the parties of the so-called war aims majority, Bethmann Hollweg declared in the Reichstag on December 9, 1914, that "neither in the east nor in the west can we allow our present enemies to control positions from which they can attack us." [6] He revealed to representatives of right-wing circles who had pressed for more specific public commitments (among them the Munich historian Marcks) that these general formulations concealed quite concrete plans:

But for the rest, I . . . could not in my speeches go beyond securing our frontiers against every danger and blocking invasion routes through Belgium and Poland. The incorporation of Bel-

5. It should be added that in the same review Herzfeld claims I wanted to write "the conclusive history of how Germany's growth was impaired by the legacy of her domestic development." He concludes that I failed in this attempt, however, "because of an approach and method that were too limited and poorly applied." I expressed my views on the matter of methodology in German historiography as early as 1963. These views were published in 1964 in the *Historische Zeitschrift* 199/2, and I have added to them in Part II of the present book. Concerning the validity of my approach, I need only point to the mass of literature my book has provoked. In response to Herzfeld's assertions, I would like to emphasize that the purpose of my book is to present German war aims policy, not to include all aspects of German policy during the First World War. A study of this kind certainly should be done now, however, to offset Ritter's book, which has once again chosen the limited perspective of studying Bethmann Hollweg's tragedy. Also, I regret that Herzfeld has replaced the fruitful concept of continuity, which he introduced into the debate in 1960, with the watered down and apologetic language of the "legacy of Germany's domestic development."

6. F. Fischer, *Griff nach der Weltmacht*, p. 265.

gium and Poland into Mitteleuropa was implied, and that is no
small aim. . . . We are keeping all the cards in our hand hid-
den from the enemy's eyes.[7]

Even if we accept Ritter's view that this was only a conciliatory gesture toward impatient zealots of world power
and therefore not to be taken seriously, the fact that Bethmann Hollweg felt compelled to make these binding promises at all shows how much he was committed to the demands of these circles. In a letter of May 5, 1915, to the
chancellor, the Pan-German advocate General von Gebsat-
tel threatened Bethmann Hollweg with a coup from the
Right. He asserted:

. . . that in its political war aims, the government has set its
sights too low. As a result, the most loyal and politically de-
pendable circles must conclude that our certain victory will not
be exploited to the full. My conscience urges me to warn
against such a course. It would be the most fateful of political
mistakes and would lead to *revolution*.[8]

As the chancellor of Germany, Bethmann Hollweg spoke
for the classes whose support was essential to the state, even
if his desires differed from theirs. He could not categori-
cally reject their demands and aims, although he modified
them according to his understanding of the immediate political and military situation. To expect Bethmann Hollweg,
in his capacity as chancellor, to have rejected war aims al-
together would be like expecting the Pope to convert to
Protestantism. Then, too, Bethmann Hollweg's relative
moderation and his ingeniously evasive formulations of all
war aims must be seen from the perspective of a chancellor
who had undertaken to insure the support of the Social
Democrats and therefore could not cast doubt on his own

7. *Ibid.*, p. 113.
8. H. Class, *Wider den Strom* (Leipzig, 1932), p. 406. Cf. A. Kruck,
Geschichte des Alldeutschen Verbandes, p. 75.

dogma of a defensive war. Although Bethmann Hollweg needed the cooperation of the Social Democrats in the war effort, very narrow limits were set to the concessions he could make to them. Loebell, the Prussian minister of the interior, who was diametrically opposed to Bethmann Hollweg in constitutional questions, defined these limits with unmatched accuracy: "The government's power ends where democracy begins: with the question of constitutional reform and of the division of domestic political power between government and popular representatives." [9] Encouraged by the Kaiser's remark that "party differences no longer divide us," the Social Democrats had believed, even before the setback at the Marne, that the time for a new orientation of domestic politics had come. In a conversation with Vice-Chancellor Delbrück shortly before September 13, 1914, the Socialist Dr. David had therefore offered to cooperate with the government in the framework of a "national democracy." Bethmann Hollweg had been willing to go along with this suggestion only on condition that the Social Democrats show "dedication to the state and to the political system the Social Democrats have habitually branded as militarism." [10] As Wahnschaffe said to the Socialist Cohen on October 2, 1914,[11] the monarchical form of government in which "the army plays such a decisive role" would have to remain unchanged. Bethmann Hollweg refused to make any immediate concessions. He would initiate the suffrage reform (which Cohen had suggested to Wahnschaffe) "only as a reward for work done," not as "payment in advance." [12]

9. Deutsches Zentralarchiv, Merseburg, Rep. 90a, Tit. I 1, no. 2, Abt. D, Bed. 1, p. 203, report of Loebell, December 21, 1915, quoted from W. Gutsche, "Bethmann Hollweg und die Politik der 'Neuorientierung,' " in *Zeitschrift für Geschichtswissenschaft,* 1965, p. 215.
10. Deutsches Zentralarchiv, Potsdam, RK, Grosses Hauptquartier 21, no. 2476, Bethmann Hollweg to Delbrück, September 19, 1914.
11. F. Fischer, *Griff nach der Weltmacht,* p. 433.
12. *Ibid.,* pp. 432 f.

Only after the defeat at the Marne and the realization that the war would not end in the autumn did the chancellor ask his representative in Berlin, Vice-Chancellor Delbrück, to announce a "new orientation," though only in vague terms. On October 21, Delbrück told the party leaders of the Prussian lower house that the national unity evident at the outbreak of the war would "affect our whole domestic policy and lead to its reorientation in many areas." [13] In a memorandum to the chancellor on October 27, 1914, Delbrück wrote that this was "perhaps the last opportunity to win" the Social Democrats "not only for the nation but also for the government. . . . The government must avoid treating the labor movement as a subversive element and must consult with its main constituency, the unions. Those dogmatists of the old school Social Democracy who are unsympathetic to the government must be given no further opportunity to lead the workers against it." [14] Consistent with Prussian tradition, this reform was to come from above before it was demanded from below.

But before any concrete suggestions could be made, these vague hints of postwar reform were sufficient to alarm and arouse conservative forces. As early as October 23, Bethmann Hollweg's trusted associate in the German chancellery, Under-Secretary Wahnschaffe, reported to him:

I have . . . the impression that forces in heavy industry and in extreme conservative circles are working against Your Excellency. They fear . . . that after the conclusion of peace excessive concessions will be made to democratic demands.[15]

13. Deutsches Zentralarchiv, Merseburg, Rep. 90a, Tit. I 1, no. 2, Abt. D, vol. 1, p. 84. Cf. W. Gutsche, *Zeitschrift für Geschichtswissenschaft*, p. 217 (October 21), and Deutsches Zentralarchiv, Potsdam, Reichskanzlei 2476, vol. I, p. 108 (October 27); cf. Gutsche, p. 216.

14. Deutsches Zentralarchiv, Potsdam, RK, Grosses Hauptquartier 21, no. 2476, vol. I, memorandum by Delbrück, October 27, 1914, quoted from Gutsche, *Zeitschrift für Geschichtswissenschaft*, p. 216.

15. K. Westarp, *Konservative Politik im letzten Jahrzehnt des Kaiserreiches*, vol. II (Berlin, 1935), p. 307.

The chancellor met with vigorous opposition from the Prussian state ministry (the Minister of the Interior and especially the Minister of Education), the Prussian bureaucracy together with the Conservative Party, and "Rhineland-Westphalian industry as well as the Pan-Germans allied with it." Hugenberg and Beumer, leaders of industrial organizations, joined forces in the Sub-Committee for the Planning of Economic and Political Aims in the Present War. Their purpose was "to divert the attention of the people from domestic reform and to free the imagination for the task of expanding German territory." [16]

Bethmann Hollweg opposed the views of the Prussian minister of the interior, Loebell, and urged that "national unity should not be sacrificed to outmoded considerations." [17] But the Kaiser was on Loebell's side; he declared himself in "complete agreement" with Loebell's memorandum of November 22, 1915, and ignored Bethmann Hollweg's hastily written memorandum of December 9, 1915. Yet Delbrück, who was concerned about the increasing influence of the Left on the labor movement, concluded as early as May 1915 that postponement of reform in all phases of domestic policy was no longer tenable. In a memorandum of May 23, 1915, on domestic reform, he had suggested to Bethmann Hollweg the following proposals for "immediate action": reform of Prussian suffrage; a change in the law governing organizations (*Vereinsgesetz*); greater freedom to form trade unions; and greater freedom of activity for existing unions, provided they raised only economic questions and renounced strike propaganda.[18] On December 11, 1915, despite continued resistance, the chancellor spoke in the Bundesrat and Reichstag, supporting a draft for an amendment to the *Vereinsgesetz*. The

16. *Ibid.*
17. Quoted according to W. Gutsche, *Zeitschrift für Geschichtswissenschaft,* p. 219. Deutsches Zentralarchiv, Merseburg, Rep. 90a, Tit. I, no. 2, Abt. D., vol. I.
18. Deutsches Zentralarchiv, Potsdam, RdI, no. 6111, Delbrück to Bethmann Hollweg, May 23, 1915.

Reichstag finally passed the amendment on June 5, 1916. Bethmann Hollweg argued that it would not be possible to keep the revisionist wing of the Social Democrats cooperative "if they were not allowed some success in the area of domestic politics." [19] He added that the revisionist Socialist leaders had not failed the government up to that point during the war. Using this same line of reasoning, the chancellor proposed on January 3 that the Crown address opening the new session of the Prussian Landtag include an announcement of suffrage reform. Helfferich supported him with the comment: "The government must insure that the radicals in the Social Democratic party do not defeat the revisionists." [20] But Bethmann Hollweg again met with bitter resistance from numerous Prussian ministers; and the Crown address, released on January 13, 1916, made only very general promises for after the war. (Only the stresses of the war year 1916, the harsh winter of 1916–17, and the shock of the Russian Revolution made it possible for the chancellor to attempt this step again. But his efforts to introduce immediate reform and equal suffrage failed once more because of opposition from the Prussian state ministry and the Conservatives. The Kaiser's Easter message of April 1917 spoke of postwar suffrage reform only in very general terms.[21])

Bethmann Hollweg hoped that the founding of the *Freie Vaterländische Vereinigung* (Union of the Free Fatherland), later renamed the *Deutsche Nationalausschuss* (German National Committee), would create broader support for his policy of domestic "re-orientation" and moderate war aims. The actual result was that the right-wing parties, heavy industry, and large groups of intellectuals joined to-

19. Deutsches Zentralarchiv, Merseburg, Rep. 90a, B III, 2b no. 6, vol. 164.
20. *Ibid.*
21. F. Fischer, *Griff nach der Weltmacht*, pp. 435 ff.; R. Patemann, *Der Kampf um die preussische Wahlreform im ersten Weltkrieg*, Düsseldorf, 1964.

gether and intensified the isolation of the chancellor, who
could not turn to the Social Democrats for support. The organizations named above were founded on Bethmann Hollweg's initiative and with government funds, but their main
backers were the banks and the electrical and oil industries
dependent on the banks. These financial pressure groups
saw their interests in central Africa and, above all, in the
east. As far as the west was concerned, they were prepared
to renounce annexations in France and Belgium and to accept Bethmann Hollweg's suggested "guarantees" for making Belgium dependent on Germany and for securing German economic influence in France. Heavy industry and the
chemical industry rejected this concentration on the east.
They wanted annexations in the west to insure Germany's
source of raw materials there as well. In their dispute with
Bethmann Hollweg, these groups could count on the army,
the aristocracy east of the Elbe, and influential groups in
the Prussian and German bureaucracy. Bethmann Hollweg's attempts at domestic reform in 1916–17 and his war
aims program failed because of this bloc. His fall in July
1917 came about not because he was too reactionary for
the new majority that supported the peace resolution but
because he was too liberal for the conservative groups. In
their view, he had capitulated to parliamentarianism. Ironi-
cally, he objected to it in principle as much as his opponents did.

At the same time that the "majority parties" joined together in their peace resolution and occasioned Bethmann
Hollweg's fall, the economic associations of industry, agriculture, and the middle classes emphatically restated their
old goals in a major petition to the government.[22] This petition, which has so far received little attention from historians, protested against the relinquishment of previous war
aims and led to a regrouping of the Center and of some lib-

22. This petition is included in the appendix to the Polish edition of I.
Geiss, *Der polnische Grenzstreifen.*

eral factions. The result was that the great majority of the parties approved the terms of Brest Litovsk. During all the negotiations for this treaty, the government was under the most severe pressure from the above-mentioned economic groups and a large segment of the German press. (And Ritter thinks *Griff nach der Weltmacht* [*Germany's Aims in the First World War*] deals with the "war aims of the German government"! [23])

But the "war aims policy of Germany" was not influenced solely by these private interest groups. There were similar groups at work within the governments and bureaucracies of the Reich and of the Bundesstaaten. Formally, the chancellor alone was responsible to the Kaiser, but it was only natural that the military, which maintained close ties with the parties, industry, and agriculture, would play a special role in wartime. In addition, numerous organizations closely linked with the economy swelled the bureaucracy during the war. These organizations played a decisive part in formulating the political goals of the chancellor and of his closest advisers. Also, overstepping the limits Bethman Hollweg's "caution" occasionally set, they defined and advocated goals shared by both political and economic leaders.

Government, bureaucracy, intellectual elite, and property owners—the landholding aristocracy and the conservative industrialists—appointed themselves representatives of "imperial Germany" and of the "nation." These groups exploited the war to maintain their own position. To what extent the interests of this "nation" coincided with those of the broad, unpropertied, and unconsulted classes is another matter. In traditional German historiography, the term "resistance" is applied exclusively to representatives of the "nation": the cautious Bethmann Hollweg; the third minister for foreign affairs, Kühlmann; and the historian Hans

23. G. Ritter, *Der erste Weltkrieg: Studien zum deutschen Geschichtsbild* (Bonn, 1964), p. 26.

Delbrück, who changed to a line of moderation. Resistance by the unorganized or organized masses at the lower levels is described as a crippling of the war effort, as treason, and as the product of a subversive ideology. For the historian, however, this resistance from below is evidence of an authoritarian pressure from above. This pressure, which increased in the course of the war, arose from attempts to strengthen the conservative system and from adherence to expansionist, imperialistic ideas.

Victory: Preservation of the Conservative System, Not Its Abolition

The expansionist war aims of Germany's political and economic forces were also designed to defend her traditional social structure against the threatening forces of democracy. In domestic policy, this meant adherence to the Prussian system of suffrage and resistance to parliamentary government in the Reich and in the individual states. In foreign policy, the tendency was, wherever possible, to place the government of occupied countries in the hands of a small group of local aristocrats, with or without a German dynasty at their head.

Above all, the position of the army in the state was to remain unquestioned. The military played a relatively large role in all countries at that time, but only in Germany were civilians subordinate to the military. And what was truly unique in this relationship was that the civilians willingly accepted their inferiority. The army and the classes supporting it hoped to retain and if possible extend this influence during the war. Thus, despite the extraordinary increase in the number of officers and reserve officers caused by the war, the army was able to preserve the social unity of the officer corps, successfully ward off all dangers of democratization until the end of the war, and maintain the military's privileged position in the state. It was able to achieve these goals because of the strength of its tradition and the consistent adherence to authority expressed in its direct responsibility to the monarch as the supreme commander. One of the main prewar concerns of the Prussian Ministry of War was to keep the proportion of aristocrats in the officer corps as high as possible. This was the reason for creating the rank of *Feldwebelleutnant* (warrant officer). Also, by establishing the OHL (*Oberste Heeresleitung*— Supreme Army Command), which had the official capacity of a general staff for the field army, the army created an instrument of ever-increasing importance in the political arena. In Ritter's moralizing view the OHL was primarily responsible for the growth of excessive militarism; [1] and it is indeed impossible to overemphasize the influence the OHL had on German war aims policy and on the first realization of that policy in the peace treaties of Brest-Litovsk and Bucharest. The OHL was able to exercise this influence, particularly after August 1916, by virtue of its own agencies and its close ties to pressure groups in the society. It had sections for politics, propaganda, and economics; and it maintained easily documented connections with elements of the Conservative Party, with the National Liberals, and with the Fatherland Party, the numerically strongest political organization the Reich produced. Most important of all were its contacts with industrial groups.

The increased influence the OHL was able to exert during the war was not, as Gerhard Ritter tries to prove, directly due to the war itself or to the efforts of that rabid "militarist" Ludendorff. It was instead a reflection of the

1. G. Ritter, *Staatskunst und Kriegshandwerk,* vol. III.

entire system. (One need think only of the Kaiser's *maison militaire*.) The conservative, pseudo-liberal forces in the Prusso-German state seemed to have lost ground in the pre-war years. The war provided an opportunity to assert and strengthen the old social and political order and to assimilate the Social Democrats as well. That was Bethmann Hollweg's task in domestic politics, and he seemed to be accomplishing it.

On August 4, 1914, the Social Democrats approved war credits; and, under pressure from the conservatives, they refrained from an anti-annexationist declaration in the Reichstag. At that point, their speaker, Dr. David, expecting a rapid victory over France, thought he could offer the government the cooperation of the revisionist wing of his party within a framework of "national democracy." He asked for a "significant gesture" from an "appropriate source" so that the revisionists could assert control over the party. In response, Bethmann Hollweg explained to the Socialists what could make cooperation possible. The conditions Bethmann Hollweg set perfectly express Germany's resolve to maintain the conservative system.[2]

The leaders of the Social Democratic Party must understand, however, that the German Reich, and particularly the Prussian state [!], can never permit any weakening of the firm foundation on which they are built: dedication to the state and to the political system the Social Democrats have habitually branded as militarism. . . . As soon as the German Left is prepared to accept the idea of a nation in arms and to adopt the national spirit behind it, a reorientation of our domestic policy will be possible.

In his essay in the *Historische Zeitschrift* 199, October 1964, Egmont Zechlin severely criticized me for "not considering this key document, although it is in the same folder

2. F. Fischer, *Griff nach der Weltmacht*, p. 432.

as the September memorandum." [3] Unfortunately, Zechlin did not read far enough in my book. Otherwise, he could not have missed the fact that in chapter XI, under the sub-title "Bethmann Hollweg and the Social Democrats," I not only quoted large sections of this document, which is indeed a key one for judging Bethmann Hollweg's domestic policies, but also offered a thorough interpretation of it.

Fastening on my alleged "failure" to consider this document, Zechlin accused me of overemphasizing the "significance of industrial interests in government thinking" and of neglecting the "importance of the counter interests of aristocratic-agrarian and bureaucratic Germany." [4] I would reply that the industrial sector of Germany gained in importance as the wartime need for industrial production increased. The longer the war lasted, the more significant German industry became for the survival of Germany and her allies. But at the same time, the importance and power of the agrarian sector also increased. Complete isolation from the world market and the consequent need for self-sufficiency led to much greater dependence on domestic agricultural production than had ever existed under prewar protective tariffs. The major East Elbian grain producers —the agrarian-conservative forces with close ties to the Prussian army—profited most from this development.

The war served the interests of both industry and agriculture, the two mainstays of conservative Prusso-Germany. It reinforced their common bonds, and they worked together in turn to preserve the existing social and political order.

Zechlin completely misunderstands the fact that Kehr's "not only/but also" view of Germany's industrial and agrarian-conservative structure does not suggest conflict between these two politically influential groups.[5] On the contrary, it reflects a merger of their interests in a dialecti-

3. E. Zechlin, *Historische Zeitschrift*, 199/2, p. 431.
4. *Ibid.*, pp. 430 ff.
5. E. Kehr, *Schlachtflottenbau und Parteipolitik* (Berlin, 1930).

cal synthesis, a merger whose goal was to stabilize and if possible to strengthen the existing social and political order. The war aims programs these groups developed jointly during the war clearly express this intention and show unequivocally what "not only/but also" means.

Industrialists like Krupp, Stinnes, Thyssen, Hugenberg, and Roetger, and their lobbyists in the Reichstag and the Prussian Landtag (Erzberger, Stresemann, and Bassermann, among others), were prepared to grant control of large areas in the east to agricultural interests. In exchange, they hoped for gains in France (annexation of Longwy-Briey and the exploitation of the French market), in Luxemburg and Belgium, in the Ukraine and Transcaucasia, in Rumania, in Rump Russia, in Turkey, and, of course, in the newly won colonies. The areas in the east, dominated either directly or indirectly by Germany, were to provide cheap labor for the East Elbian estates and land for colonization by German farmers and war veterans. The "inner colonization" that large landowners considered a serious threat would thus be channeled to eastern Europe, and at the same time, the "base of support for the state" would be broadened.[6]

The joint efforts of these two groups also proved "effective" in preventing any conceivable reform of Prussian suffrage and in warding off the "danger" of a democratization of Prussia. In the summer of 1917, the National Liberals in the Reichstag had been willing to make some concessions on the suffrage question (along lines suggested by Max Weber [7]) in order to raise the morale of the masses and increase their contribution to the war effort. But, like the Center Party delegates who supported the peace resolution,[8] the National Liberals in the Reichstag were repudiated by the party's executive committees at both the national and state level. The conservative National Liberals

6. F. Fischer, *Griff nach der Weltmacht*, pp. 714 ff. and 809 ff.
7. M. Weber, *Politische Schriften*.
8. F. Fischer, *Griff nach der Weltmacht*, pp. 561 ff.

in the Prussian Abgeordnetenhaus were closely linked to industry and were particularly adamant in their opposition to their colleagues in the Reichstag. Despite the Kaiser's Easter message and the "alarming" promise which Bethmann Hollweg had wrung from him in July 1917,[9] the Prussian Landtag managed to have the decision on suffrage reform postponed until after the war. What the decision would have been was clearly demonstrated in the spring of 1918, when the Prussian Abgeordnetenhaus voted down the reform. At that time, the German offensive in the west promised victory; and concessions to the masses no longer seemed necessary. The Prussian Herrenhaus, representing the landed aristocracy, heavy industry, high finance, and the Prussian bureaucracy, was even less receptive to the proposed change.[10]

The struggle over the suffrage question made Bethmann Hollweg's isolation clear and showed that any policy based on Social Democratic support was doomed to failure. In the summer of 1917, the prospect of American intervention in the war seemed to be increasing the war-weariness of the masses and weakening their determination to fight on to total victory. Concerned about this and about the impact of the Russian Revolution, Bethmann Hollweg urged the Kaiser to proclaim that equal, direct, and secret voting would be adopted in Prussia after the war; but the Prussian state ministry stood united against him. Led by the Prussian minister of the interior, Loebell, the ministry defended the character of the Prussian state, based on agrarian-feudal and middle-class values, against the bureaucrat Bethmann Hollweg, with his "liberal egghead" ideas. As a result, only a very vague promise of postwar reform was made.[11]

As early as the spring of 1917, war aims had become

9. *Ibid.*, pp. 516 ff.
10. H. Thieme, *Nationaler Liberalismus in der Krise: Die national-liberale Fraktion des preussischen Abgeordnetenhauses 1914–18,* Dissertation, University of Hamburg, 1962, Schriften des Bundesarchivs, vol. 11 (Hamburg, 1963).
11. F. Fischer, *Griff nach der Weltmacht,* pp. 521 f.

closely tied to this domestic issue. The Kreuznach conference of April 1917, the Austro-German conferences in which Austria-Hungary had to submit to German wishes, and the soundings for a separate peace with Russia all made this connection eminently clear. But, most important, this interplay between war aims and domestic political reform played a crucial role in the crisis of July 1917 that ended in Bethmann Hollweg's dismissal. "Discouraged" by the lack of progress in the war and by the disappointing results of unlimited U-boat warfare, Bethmann Hollweg urged the Kaiser not only to promise equal suffrage, which could go into effect either immediately or after the war, but also to show some flexibility in the matter of war aims.[12] With these efforts, Bethmann Hollweg wrote his own death sentence. He had overstepped the limits that made him acceptable to the controlling interests of Germany. Deference to these interests is essential for a chief of state, not adherence to an abstract *raison d'état,* as Ritter would have us believe. The fall of the "war chancellor," Bethmann Hollweg, rich in intrigue, has often been told, most recently by Gerhard Ritter.[13] But however fascinating this incident may be for a historian with a penchant for drama, it is of little value to a historical assessment as long as it is seen in isolation. It has to be amplified by an objective study of the forces that caused Bethmann Hollweg's fall and of the interests they represented. This subject is not exhausted by calling attention to the "foolish" and "incomprehensible" behavior of the "opportunist" Erzberger and of the "stupid" Social Democrats. Nor is it exhausted by branding as "militarism" what should properly be called violations of the constitution on the part of the generals and the Crown Prince. An objective study of this subject requires nothing more nor less than an investigation of the balance of power within Germany.

12. *Ibid.,* pp. 522 ff.
13. G. Ritter, *Staatskunst und Kriegshandwerk,* vol. III, pp. 492 ff.

Bethmann Hollweg was tolerated as long as he pursued the aims of the ruling social and political classes. He did so by keeping the Social Democrats cooperative and, even more important, by keeping them in their place. His other function was to act as spokesman for a "good" and "moderate" Germany in case peace overtures proved necessary. But he was no longer needed when he seemed to have lost control over the Social Democrats and when American entry into the war put an end to his role as a possible spokesman for peace—indeed, made this role seem dangerous to Germany. His successor, Michaelis, did not bring the necessary abilities to the office and was simply a tool of the right-wing parties and of the OHL. Count Hertling, Michaelis' successor, could always rely on support from one state (Bavaria) and from at least the conservative wing of one major party (the Center). Like Bethmann Hollweg, he was a convinced adherent of constitutional monarchy and a spokesman for the classes supporting it. With the backing of these forces, Hertling succeeded during his chancellorship in resisting all efforts to extend parliamentary government in the Reich and in the individual states, especially in Prussia. Like Bethmann Hollweg, he was prepared to make certain concessions in the matter of Prussian suffrage, but he did not think he could put the reform through against the opposition to it in Prussia. Nor was he particularly eager to put it through. Then, too, as chancellor, Hertling was formally responsible for the peace treaties of Brest Litovsk and Bucharest, which are often unjustifiably attributed to the OHL alone. Like the minister of foreign affairs, von Kühlmann, Hertling was more interested in keeping the structure of German domination in eastern Europe flexible than in making the terms of the treaties more moderate.

These peace treaties were approved by all the Reichstag parties except the Majority Socialists, who abstained, and the numerically small Independent Socialists, who opposed. Wilson had regarded the Social Democrats as the main representatives of the "other" Germany, but their vote on this matter—indeed, the vote of all the parties—prompted him to drop this distinction between government and people, between the Germany of militarism and imperialism and the "other" Germany,[14] and to continue the war until Germany was defeated.

The "nation" greeted the peace of Brest Litovsk with enthusiastic expressions of confidence in victory. The few voices of criticism or reservation remained unheard. Zechlin makes much of long-overdue doubts that Bethmann Hollweg revealed in a letter to Prince Max of Baden,[15] but in the face of such popular enthusiasm these doubts are of little significance. The *Allgemeine Evangelisch-Lutherische Kirchenzeitung* reflected the feelings of the nation:

Peace without annexations and reparations! Such was man's resolve. . . . But here, too, God willed otherwise. . . . And Russia, which was determined not to pay reparations, finally had to give up immense booty: 800 locomotives and 8,000 railroad cars filled with all manner of goods and provisions. God knew we needed this. We also needed cannons and munitions for the final thrust against the enemy in the west. God knew that, too. So out of His generosity—for God is rich—He gave us 2,600 cannons, 5,000 machine guns, 2 million rounds of ammunition for the artillery. He also gave us rifles, airplanes, trucks, and much more.[16]

This peace settlement deprived Russia of one third of her agricultural production and 70 percent of her coal and ore yield.[17] From Finland to Georgia, it created a chain of buffer states dependent on Germany. Germany had realized her war aims. The treaty gave German industry the great markets it desired, including Rump Russia, and abundant

14. See the dissertation of my student J. Möckelmann.
15. Reprinted in E. Zechlin, *Historische Zeitschrift,* 199/2, pp. 451–58.
16. F. Fischer, *Griff nach der Weltmacht,* p. 672.
17. *Ibid.,* p. 643.

sources of raw materials. Again, policy aims had been fulfilled. The treaty also strengthened agrarian-feudal Germany by extending the monarchical idea and driving back revolutionary Russia. Germany and Austria-Hungary, autocratic in structure and dominated by monarchy and church, relied on various measures to guarantee the dependence of the newly acquired areas. They planned to establish German dynasties in Finland, the Baltic states, Lithuania, Poland, and possibly the Ukraine and Georgia. They hoped to draw the upper Polish aristocracy, the Polish church, and, especially, the Lithuanian church into their sphere of influence; and they counted on the support of the German aristocracy in the Baltic states. By stressing the need to combat "Bolshevism," Germany capitalized on the economic interests of the agricultural middle class in the occupied territories and lent an appearance of ideological justification to her power aspirations. The government and the OHL transformed Germany's desires for power into a European mission: Germany pre-empted the role of defender of the "Western heritage." Under the slogan of the "ideas of 1914" [18] the people were indoctrinated with Germany's special task and mission in the war. These "ideas of 1914" were diametrically opposed to the ideas of 1789. German professors and journalists formulated the theory of the uniqueness of the German state and society, and they claimed that German spirit and culture were as distinct from Russian tyranny as they were from western European democracy. The conservative, Lutheran view of the state, the evocation of the Germanic warrior and of the Iron Chancellor Bismarck, and the postulation of a "German God" [19] by Max Lenz all combined in an ideological enhancement of the war and lent to it a religious consecration

18. R. Kjellén, "Die Ideen von 1914," *Zwischen Krieg und Frieden* (Leipzig, 1915), Heft 29.
19. M. Lenz, "Der deutsche Gott," *Süddeutsche Monatshefte*, September 1914.

reflected in the phrase the "German war." According to the "ideas of 1914," this was not a struggle for power but a struggle of the German spirit against the forces of democracy in the west and of barbarism in the east. Here, heightened by the fact of war, ideas that generations of German theologians, humanists, and economists had propounded to create a national consciousness became relevant once more.

Two factors strengthened the determination of the anti-democratic and anti-parliamentarian forces behind the conservative Prusso-German church and monarchy. One was the transformation of tsarist, panslavistic Russia—the nation that had been considered the one great threat before the war—into Lenin's bolshevistic, revolutionary Russia. The other was the declared intention of the democratic forces, first stated by England, then by Wilson speaking for America, to combat autocracy and Prusso-German militarism. This background is essential to an understanding of Germany's efforts not just to maintain but to extend a "Germanic" world between the "Slavic" order on her one frontier and "Romance and Anglo-Saxon" civilization on the other. Germany's sense of mission—and her isolation between east and west—is clearly expressed in a speech the Kaiser gave on June 15, 1918, when Germany was experiencing her last surge of confidence in victory just one month before the great reversals in the west.

Either Germanic ideals or Anglo-Saxon ones must prevail. Justice, freedom, honor, and virtue will triumph, or the worship of money. There can be only one victor in this struggle. German ideals are at stake![20]

The purpose of Germany's war policy was to impose her "ideals" on the world. This ultimate aim cannot be regarded as a tactical goal or an annexationist dream. It was a genuine expression of Germany's demands for power and "security."

20. F. Fischer, *Griff nach der Weltmacht*, p. 838.

PART TWO

In Response to Methodological Criticism

In August 1964 the Südwestfunk broadcast four lectures by Gerhard Ritter. In the fall of the same year, these radio talks appeared in the "Schriftenreihe der Bundeszentrale für politische Bildung," collected under the title *Der erste Weltkrieg: Studien zum deutschen Geschichtsbild,*[1] and were distributed free of charge to all West German history teachers. In these lectures, Ritter suggests that "our national historical consciousness" would be still further "darkened" ("even more than it was by the experiences of the Hitler period") if it were true that Germany did not just "ineptly" stumble into World War I and if it were true that Germany pursued goals during the war that were not of a purely defensive nature. For if Germany did in fact exploit the murder at Sarajevo as a golden opportunity to declare war, as I have argued in my book *Griff nach der Weltmacht* (*Germany's Aims in the First World War*) and in essays written before and after it, and if Germany did fight the war to expand her hegemony, this knowledge could, according to the "old master of political historians," "prove dangerous . . . for the political consciousness of the nation."

But what does it mean to say this could "prove dangerous"? How can a rational, objective judgment of the German past, corroborated by international scholarship, "prove dangerous"? Does Ritter mean, perhaps, that this kind of historical judgment in some way fosters "nihilistic tendencies" in Germany's student population? Does he mean that emphasizing Germany's guilt, or at least her great share of guilt, for the First World War (as well as for the Second) could encourage resistance to the draft? Does he mean that the assessment of Germany's power aspirations as realities and not as annexationist fantasies could evoke national resignation? He apparently means all this. For wherever decisions involving power politics are concerned,

---

1. G. Ritter, *Der erste Weltkrieg: Studien zum deutschen Geschichtsbild,* Schriftenreihe der Bundeszentrale für Politische Bildung, Heft 65 (Bonn, 1964). See also G. Ritter, *Historische Zeitschrift,* 194 (1962), pp. 646 f.

Ritter sees Fate at work; wherever defeats can be established in objective terms, Ritter speaks of tragedy; and where we today see incongruities and where it is impossible to overlook disastrous decisions that were made, there Ritter tells us we must show understanding. No matter how hard he may try, Ritter, a true son of Germany under the Kaiser, evidently finds it impossible to come to a rational, unemotional judgment.

With the sovereign tone for which he has always been admired, Ritter condemns me and my work for a "regrettable degree of prejudice and for an inability to penetrate the historical situation. . . . This can only be regarded as the worst kind of tendentious historiography." [2] But after looking closely at the documents and at Ritter's work, we can and must level this same criticism at him. Ritter's book on Luther and his work on Machiavelli and More show that his career has been one of political history, of tendentious historiography. His most recent book, *Staatskunst und Kriegshandwerk III, Die Tragödie der Staatskunst: Bethmann Hollweg als Kriegskanzler,* 1964 (*The Sword and the Scepter*), is in this same vein. The lectures I mentioned above clearly illustrate Ritter's intellectual tradition, the tradition of apologetic journalism and historiography which began in 1914 or 1918 and which regarded it as a national duty not to clarify and analyze but to justify, or at least "understand," the evolution and the actions of the Prusso-German national state, a tradition that also took it upon itself to provide models of political and military leadership rather than to conduct objective investigations of the past.

But however much the work of the historian may affect the historical and political consciousness of the present, historical truth should never be made dependent on a traditional view or a "binding" heritage. Nor should it be guided by a political ideal, as Ritter believes it must, in order to preserve for the German Federal Republic the glorious *raison d'état* tradition of Bismarck, Bethmann Hollweg, and Stresemann. Germany's thousand-year history cannot be understood solely from the perspective of the fifty-year Bismarck Reich, and four-fifths of German history during the First World War unfortunately do

---

2. G. Ritter, *Staatskunst und Kriegshandwerk,* vol. III, p. 596, note 60.

not fit into Ritter's image of this Bismarck tradition. Ritter's third volume, although he certainly did not intend it as such, is clear proof of my point, because, despite his efforts, he cannot interpret away Bethmann Hollweg's failure ("the tragedy of statesmanship") which resulted from the chancellor's conflict with the will of the "nation."

Egmont Zechlin's approach is less obvious in its motivation and is apparently prompted by scholarly concerns quite different from Ritter's. Zechlin speaks in terms of "continuity in German strategy" and of Bethmann Hollweg's "cabinet war." Because of England's unexpected response, Bethmann Hollweg's "cabinet war" took on a different character. England, that perfidious Albion, reacted to Bethmann Hollweg's "masterpiece of diplomacy" as if this diplomatic action carried the threat of a war for hegemony. Zechlin's position is not easy to define since each publication (and he has published extensively) presents a new thesis and a new approach. At first his catchword was "revolutionization," then "separate peace," then "cabinet war." [3] One eagerly awaits his next inspiration. But other idiosyncrasies complicate an understanding of Zechlin's thesis even more. He contradicts himself in each work, makes facile combinations, loses the thread of his argument while examining a document, and creates parallels which lie less in the material than in his own mental constructs. Furthermore, his work (especially his article in the *Historische Zeitschrift* of October 1964) is characterized by a fitfulness which leads him to raise questions that do not add to his argument. But putting these lapses and discrepancies aside, one recognizes that Zechlin's thinking (so far, at least) revolves around two poles: first, the German government only reacted to English provocations;

---

3. E. Zechlin, "Friedensbestrebungen und Revolutionierungsversuche," Beilagen zu: *Das Parlament*, B 20/61, B 24/61, B 25/61, B 20/63, and B 22/63; E. Zechlin, "Das 'schlesische Angebot' und die italienische Kriegsgefahr," *Geschichte in Wissenschaft und Unterricht*, 14 (1963), pp. 533 ff.; E. Zechlin, "Deutschland zwischen Kabinettskrieg und Wirtschaftskrieg: Politik und Kriegsführung in den ersten Monaten des Weltkrieges 1914," *Historische Zeitschrift*, 199 (1964), pp. 347 ff.; E. Zechlin, "Probleme des Kriegskalküls und der Kriegsbeendigung im ersten Weltkrieg," *Geschichte in Wissenschaft und Unterricht*, 16 (1965), pp. 69 ff.

and, second, the German government had no political aims whatsoever before or even during the war. German policy was no more than a response to "outside pressures."

Thus, Zechlin can pursue any interpretation he likes without fear of stumbling over realities that might lie in his path. For him, even if he does not admit it, England (and sometimes Russia) is the villain of Germany history. In contrast to Ritter's overemotional rehearsing of fate, Zechlin's work seems more objective and specific. A careful study of the sources, however, shows that his theory of continuity in German strategy, his distinctions (often specious), and his method all lead to an impressionistic, distorted rendering of documents and events.

EGMONT ZECHLIN:

The Theory of English
War Guilt Revived

> The most dangerous falsehoods
> are truths slightly distorted.
> *Georg Christian Lichtenberg*

A few examples will illustrate what Zechlin and Ritter call method. A classic instance of Zechlin's art of interpretation appears in the *Parlamentsbeilage* B20/63 of May 15, 1963, a study of Germany's efforts to force Russian withdrawal from the war either by concluding a separate peace with Russia or by "revolutionizing" her. Zechlin himself characterizes his own method best when he writes: "The reader will have recognized how contradictory and difficult every political decision [made by the German government] was and, consequently, how contradictory and difficult an account of such decisions must be." Zechlin did not manage in this article, as he would in later ones, to reconcile his view of a purely defensive attitude on the part of the German government with documentation that proves just the opposite. The sources show that Germany was "prepared to risk war" in July 1914, as Zechlin expresses it (or, as Riezler puts it, "willing to go to war"); and the sources also show that Germany followed an expansionist policy during the war itself. Zechlin is apparently not troubled at the thought of a government "embarking upon" a war it was convinced could not be won. Such an act would not have been mere bungling, as has been previously assumed, nor would it have been a conscious decision to achieve a position of power by means of war, as I believe it was. It would have been nothing short of murder. Both Zechlin's and Ritter's presentations show this inconsistency of interpreting German policy as basically defensive despite undeniable offensive actions.

Ritter is dismayed by "extreme criticism of the German character," asks for "understanding," wants to avoid "criticizing the German government," is personally engaged, and hopes to cast some light into the "dark corners" of German history. In contrast, Zechlin is more detached and sketches a new theory of German war policy. In the essay mentioned above, Zechlin takes the following approach to prove his theory: He is ready to accept any evidence that emphasizes the defensive aspect of Bethmann Hollweg's position, even if that evidence is drawn from Bethmann Hollweg's own memoirs (*op. cit.*, p. 8); but evidence that clearly indicates an expansionist policy is inexplicably judged "as not compelling" (*op. cit.*, pp. 16 f.). Or in a polemic tone, Zechlin creates the impression that excessive war aims, such as the annexation of the Flemish coast, were forced upon Bethmann Hollweg. Zechlin thus allows Bethmann Hollweg's efforts at compromise to appear in a favorable light. But the whole argument is untenable because no one ever imputed these particular war aims to Bethmann Hollweg.[1] This tactic of creating artificial conflicts among German leaders becomes even clearer in Zechlin's interpretation of the cabinet meeting of April 10, 1915. Here Zechlin presents us with a Bethmann Hollweg whose essentially defensive policy was a response to the "attack" of July 1914.

1. E. Zechlin, *Das Parlament,* B 20/63, p. 7.

In contrast to Zechlin's other publications, this essay accepts uncritically the argument that Germany had been "forced into war," that she had been forced "to defend her position in the world." Judging the meeting of April 1915 from this perspective, Zechlin depicts Bethmann Hollweg as concerned only with defending Germany against the superior power of the aggressors and with bringing her through the war "in a viable state."

But Zechlin avoids mentioning how and by what means this "more viable state" was to be achieved. Instead, he creates the impression that Bethmann Hollweg's skepticism about possible annexations is further evidence of a defensive policy. But this is a deception. Even Zechlin cannot claim that the failure to make annexations necessarily indicates a renunciation of annexationist desires, especially in Bethmann Hollweg's case. Zechlin is forced to grant that Bethmann Hollweg regarded "the struggle for German self-preservation" as more than that. It was also to be a means of "transforming and reordering the balance of power among nations" (*op. cit.*, p. 8), i.e., Bethmann Hollweg was thinking in terms of war aims as well as of war means. Even Zechlin admits that "from the outbreak of war until his resignation" the German chancellor persisted in the "hope" that Germany would emerge from this war secure from future attacks and with greater political and economic mobility. He could unfortunately do no more than hope, since Germany had not been victorious. But the treaty of Brest Litovsk shows that if Germany had been victorious, she would have realized Bethmann Hollweg's "hope" to the full. In practical terms Bethmann Hollweg's "hope" was identical with his concept of Mitteleuropa. If Germany had won, Mitteleuropa would have meant a reorganization of the European political order with Germany in a predominant position. This must have been regarded as a war aim at the time, and it implied demands that even Zechlin cannot seriously dispute. The character of the war changed completely after the battle of the Marne, and it is no surprise that "renunciation" rather than victory was uppermost in people's minds. It is wrong to judge Bethmann Hollweg's initial war aims on the basis of his revised aims after the Marne. To do so overlooks what I consider to be the central question: What did Germany want to accomplish if she had won a quick victory on the western front?

Zechlin also has no desire to examine the historical concept of Mitteleuropa or my use of it. For him, Mitteleuropa is essentially an economic term. But limiting the concept in this way is not permissible because the economic aspect is only one of many in this complex war aim of the German government. Furthermore, the limited material in Potsdam, which Zechlin examined after I did, does not provide an adequate understanding of the concept. Essential as this material is for comprehending the calculation of German war aims, it is distorted by the context in which Zechlin places it. This is particularly noticeable in Zechlin's analysis of how the Mitteleuropa idea was dropped. His views on this subject appeared for the first time in the *Historische Zeitschrift,* were repeated at the 1964 German Historical Convention in Berlin, and had the distinction of being reprinted in K. D. Erdmann's periodical for teachers of history.

Zechlin's argument is as follows: Sarajevo occurred at a critical moment in Anglo-German relations.[2] Since "in a few years [Russia] could no longer be contained," [3] Germany accepted "the risk of war" in order to improve her own position and that of her ally Austria-Hungary through a *fait accompli* against Serbia. Zechlin claims that England intended to oppose Germany; and according to him and Erdmann, the German government knew this. (If this were so, Ritter's criticism of England's hesitancy during the July crisis of 1914 would be unfounded.) In this way, "a

2. E. Zechlin, *Geschichte in Wissenschaft und Unterricht,* 16, p. 72.
3. *Ibid.,* p. 73 (from Riezler's diary, entry for July 7, 1914).

diplomatic offensive escalated into a world war." Zechlin clearly regrets that this second "Benedetti affair" was not as well prepared as the first one had been in 1870, when England did remain neutral. The possible use of the military had been calculated into this diplomatic offensive, and the military was in fact used "at the least inopportune" moment, according to a statement of September 13, 1914, "to counteract developments that were felt to be a threat to Germany's survival." Zechlin contends but does not prove that German leaders—Wilhelm II, Bethmann Hollweg, Zimmermann, Stumm, Müller, Reichardt, Johannes, "almost all the departments involved," Valentini, Müller, Falkenhayn, Tirpitz, Pohl, Helfferich, Rathenau, Ballin, and Gwinner —knew that they could not win this war and therefore must have fought to lose. Consequently, the German leaders hoped to wage a controlled "cabinet war" to prevent complete and final encirclement (also in military terms), since a "diplomatic retreat was considered a dishonorable capitulation." [4] Although he clearly recognizes that the undeniable German willingness to go to war contradicts him, Zechlin comes to the conclusion that Germany was "attacked."

But he found a *deus ex machina* close at hand. Germany saw the war as "an intermezzo after which the traditional policies of the great powers would be taken up again—but with the *minor change* that Germany's position would be the most auspicious possible." "The unrestricted play of diplomatic power among the leading nations," Zechlin tells us, "was expected to resume after the war."

This view runs counter to the facts. German political, military, and economic leaders sought to prevent the resumption of this "unrestricted play" in which contemporary Germans thought prewar Germany had held a role incommensurate with her human and economic power. The term

4. *Ibid.*

"minor change" both includes and conceals Germany's goals. The "most auspicious possible" position would bring with it the "minor change" that Germany would never again "be threatened." Thus, the whole problem of German war aims policy is contained in the phrase "minor change" —a change so minor that it could dictate the terms of Brest Litovsk and would have meant German domination of central Europe and central Africa.

But let us return to Zechlin. He thinks that the lawyer Bethmann Hollweg's faith in international law, which Germany had disregarded, led him to assume the risk of war, a war that "informed circles" knew "well before the defeat at the Marne could not be won against England and Russia, even if a six-week campaign against France were successful." According to Zechlin, Bethmann Hollweg anxiously sought to keep the "slaughter" to a minimum. Germany had no great ambitions—only the modest ones of self-defense and of re-establishing the prewar *status quo*. A show of German weakness was to demonstrate to the English that Germany was the main guardian of the European balance of power. This same show of weakness was to bring home to Tirpitz and the military men that they should make their peace with the Social Democrats. If this "declaration of weakness" did not achieve its purpose, then an appropriate show of strength, a victory over France, would "persuade" England to re-establish the old diplomatic interplay among the great powers.

But England would not cooperate. England interpreted "Germany's actions as a move toward hegemony and answered justifiably [whatever Zechlin means by "justifiably"] with a hegemonic war." [5] England did not escalate the German continental "cabinet war" into a world war. She simply misunderstood Bethmann Hollweg's objective by "responding" to the German "cabinet war" as if Ger-

5. *Ibid.*, pp. 75 f.

many's march through Belgium were a direct threat to England and her interests, as if the defeat of France would upset the old European order, and as if the execution of the Schlieffen plan were a challenge to England's hegemony. In Zechlin's view, the intention of German policy was simply to restore the European balance of power. Zechlin, adhering to the tradition of *toujours en vedette,* finds that Germany had merely acted on the "self-evident right of all great powers to resort to arms when it seemed to serve their interests." [6] But cannot the same be said of England?

As we mentioned before, Zechlin believes England misunderstood "this right," sent her expeditionary corps to France in mid-August, published Bethmann Hollweg's reference to a treaty of international law as a "scrap of paper," precluded the possibility of separate peace treaties, and thereby forced Germany to prolong the war. Now, according to Zechlin, Germany had to take measures against England, "the unconquerable enemy." On September 9, "a group drafted and typed" a confused catalogue of these measures. "Their work was hasty yet thorough and was carried on amid lively discussion." These measures were also to serve as conditions for an "interim peace" with France if events took the "happy turn" [!] of a victory at the Marne. Thus, Zechlin admits that the German leaders had war aims after all, even if they called them conditions for an interim peace. "Everything which could possibly be considered a desirable war aim" was to be "explored" by the staff.[7] Zechlin does not analyze the reason why "the staff in Berlin from Delbrück on down" was to explore "all these possibilities to insure that everything would work out," nor does Zechlin ask what "working out" would have meant. Bethmann Hollweg accepted the conversion, by "his enemies," of his catalogue of war means into a program of war aims; for, according to Zechlin, it was only in

6. E. Zechlin, *Historische Zeitschrift,* 199/2, p. 351.
7. E. Zechlin, *Das Parlament,* B 20/63, p. 18.

the period between August 27 and September 6 that Bethmann Hollweg "realized with dismay the unexpectedly threatening nature of the war." [8] This was the same Bethmann Hollweg who, as early as July, had spoken of a "leap in the dark"; who, at the beginning of August, had seen his policy collapse "like a house of cards"; and who, before the war, had conceived of a new political order. This is an entirely new chronology which is justified less by historical facts than by Zechlin's desire to contrive, contrary to all evidence, a defensive German policy.

Of the measures in this catalogue, Zechlin considers Mitteleuropa the principal one that was to be used against England in view of the anticipated victory over France. But he understands Mitteleuropa only as an economic union of "west-central Europe for the purpose of taking the offensive against England and putting pressure on her." Zechlin is not disquieted by the fact that the "text of the September memorandum itself expresses only covertly . . . the true intent of the Mitteleuropa plan. The plan was to take the form of a new Napoleonic blockade of the continent and was meant to serve as the initial phase of a campaign against England." [9] Zechlin is not disquieted by this fact because he thinks this "initial phase," this "main means of war," lost its tactical significance as early as September 19 and was dropped because of the opposition of Delbrück and the departments. Thus, in Zechlin's view, after adhering to it for fifteen or twenty days, Bethmann Hollweg renounced his most important "means of war"—and his most important one against the English blockade in particular!

Before discussing the letter of September 19, 1914, which Zechlin emphasizes so much as marking the end of the Mitteleuropa scheme, I would like to take a quick look at the alternative of a customs union or commercial treaties.

8. E. Zechlin, *Geschichte in Wissenschaft und Unterricht*, 16 (1965), p. 76.
9. E. Zechlin, *Historische Zeitschrift*, 199, p. 424.

Zechlin accuses me of not seeing this alternative and charges me with the "serious fault" of neglecting crucial economic considerations after the blockade. But the burden of proving the importance of this alternative for the interpretation of war aims policy lies on him. Instead of proving it, he postulates *a priori* a "harmless" continuation of prewar trade policy and regards my discussion as an *"a priori"* equation of the customs union with war aims. If he had read my book, he would have recognized how relevant for me the connection between trade policy and the customs union was—not, however, in terms of offense or defense but in terms of influence and the securing of power, considerations that formed the basis for all Prusso-German decisions on trade policy. Zechlin's only mention of the problem of world versus domestic markets occurs in a title heading. He does not pursue the question further because he believes it was no longer relevant after ten days, i.e., by September 19, since Germany had not found access to the world market or an alternative to it. Contrary to Zechlin, I consider the persistence of this problem evidence for the continuity of a German war aims policy in which the establishment of a "German trade system" is of the highest importance. I have in mind here the treaty of Brest Litovsk as well as the ideas and plans of von dem Bussche and von Stein.

Here again Zechlin deals with a question that actually existed but not in the way he perceives it. In the times of Bismarck, Caprivi, and Bülow, and in 1914 as well, trade agreements or a customs union in central Europe had always been two sides of the same coin—securing the optimum position for the German economy in Europe and in the world.[10] New opportunities and needs for a customs union opened up during the war, less because of the direct confrontation with England (although that was also involved) than because of the terms for peace that were to es-

10. See Helmut Böhme, *Deutschlands Weg zur Grossmacht,* for a study of these factors in the 1880s.

tablish Germany as a world power equal to other world powers once the expected rapid victory had been won. Mitteleuropa was to be the cornerstone of these terms. Of course, a hasty glance into one document from a whole file of hundreds of volumes cannot yield such an interpretation. A presentation of German trade policy requires a thorough examination of this material and would go beyond the scope of our study of war aims policy.

Now we must consider the letter of September 19, 1914. This key document, which I supposedly did not examine in my admittedly very long book, *Griff nach der Weltmacht* (*Germany's Aims in the First World War*), proves to be highly questionable evidence for the discontinuation of plans for a customs union. Furthermore, it is the only evidence for Bethmann Hollweg's renunciation of the customs union. Zechlin asserts that on September 19 Bethmann Hollweg "accepted . . . Delbrück's serious objections" to the customs union and "insisted only" that "the basic idea . . . of facilitating German exports should be retained—possibly on the basis of a special 'export list' of the main export products as defined in trade agreements." [11]

But the document conveys a different impression. Bethmann Hollweg in no way "accepted" the "serious objections to the customs union." He only went so far as to say he "did not deny the difficulties which would confront such a radical re-orientation." That is, the typically cautious Bethmann Hollweg recognized the difficulties which would arise from the realization of the plan. Nonetheless, he wanted to retain the "basic idea." This "basic idea" was not, as Zechlin claims, "facilitating German exports—possibly on the basis of a special 'export list' " but rather the establishment of a "unified economic area." A "list including our own main products" was to be compiled, and "minimum tariffs" would be imposed on the competing products of "the other

11. E. Zechlin, *Historische Zeitschrift*, 199, pp. 479 ff.

countries" in the union to compensate for the possible disadvantages of an abrupt removal of customs barriers. Bethmann Hollweg made this suggestion so that the political advantages of "a unified economic area" (i.e., "the basic idea") would not be immediately counteracted by the competition of Hungarian agricultural products and French wine, the traditional stumbling blocks for German trade policy. It should be kept in mind that in this document Bethmann Hollweg does not call for the "end of plans for a customs union" or reject "Rathenau's plan for a customs union." Instead, the limited concept of such a union for central Europe, a "basic idea" Bethmann Hollweg felt "should be retained," was modified to avoid disadvantages and obviate departmental objections which could arise now, after the Marne.

Zechlin's claim that the customs union "plan was dropped" is not only wrong but is also argued so ingeniously that it completely destroys his own theory of war means and, consequently, the point of departure for his whole analysis. Zechlin's title "The Dilemma of German Policy: War Means or War Aims" reflects less the dilemma of the German government than Zechlin's own. In his effort to find a middle road between Ritter and me, he loses his way completely.

Critical evaluation of Zechlin's presentation reveals distortion of this document at the most basic level of historical exegesis and clearly shows that he imposes a preconceived interpretation on historical sources. How untenable this procedure is becomes clear to us if we place the document in question in the context of a historical development that has been studied analytically and perceived in its dialectical ramifications, a development in which the political, economic, intellectual, military, and social spheres are regarded as equal factors in the historical process. I reject the method of intellectual empathy which neglects context and concentrates on isolated elements in a given historical situation, and I reject as well a method that is no more than a mere amassing of facts.

Taking still another of Zechlin's analyses, I would like to demonstrate how his reconstruction disregards the overall context and deprives a document of its significance. At the German Historical Convention in Berlin in 1964, this particular item was offered as criticism of me. The periodical *Geschichte in Wissenschaft und Unterricht* promptly published the piece without critically evaluating it at all.[12]

The subject is a marginal note of June 9, 1914, in which Wilhelm II gives the order "Clarify relations with England!" Zechlin claims this quote is of "major importance" for my central thesis of continuity in German policy, a continuity that can be traced from the "world policy" of the mid-eighteen-nineties to the July crisis of 1914 and beyond that into a "war aims policy" after August 1914. Since Zechlin regards my interpretation of this note as incorrect, he concludes that my "approach based on it is also incorrect" and, therefore, my main thesis as well.

The starting point for Zechlin's criticism is a typographical error: I referred to a file as "Turkey 169" instead of "168." According to Zechlin I had not noticed that the document belonged under "Relations of Turkey with Greece" (168) and not under "Relations of Turkey with France" (169). Zechlin believes I took the document out of its specific context and unjustifiably placed it in the general context of German policy toward England. In the first place, it is unacceptable to exaggerate the importance of a typographical error to this extent when no conclusions are based on the mistake. To be sure, all diplomatic reports are filed according to their general subject matter. Wangenheim's report does indeed concern Greek-Turkish relations and is therefore in file 168. But in this case the general subject matter is not as important as Zechlin makes it.

12. E. Zechlin, *Geschichte in Wissenschaft und Unterricht*, 16, pp. 69 ff.

Proof of my point here is the fact that a copy of the critical sentence in the Kaiser's marginal note was filed in the series "England 78" and thereby, if one will, removed from the original subject heading. This filing under two headings justifies our relating this marginal note to German policy toward England and shows that the note had particular political significance for Germany's England policy. So much for the question of "subject matter." Zechlin also emphasizes that I have not quoted the complete marginal note, the first paragraph of which deals specifically with Turko-Greek difficulties and the second of which expresses the Kaiser's opinions on the general implications of the Balkan conflicts. Since Zechlin claims to have seen the original document, he ought to have noticed that the second part of the Kaiser's comment is in a separate paragraph and is broader, more general, and consciously set off from the specific content of the first part.

If one grasps the inner organization of the Kaiser's comment, one recognizes that "to clarify" does not mean to come to an agreement with England over vital mutual interests in the partitioning of Turkey. The word "clarify" does not follow the comment in the first paragraph about "partitioning Turkey." Instead—and this is the crucial point—it follows the Kaiser's expressed anticipation of an imminent Balkan conflict.

In addition, "to clarify" does not mean to determine the position England would take if a partition of Turkey were to occur after a third Balkan war. It means that England's position should be clarified precisely because the Kaiser expected such a war "in which we shall all become involved."

Thirdly, Wilhelm II wanted to clarify relations with England not because of his vital interests in Turkey but because of "the assiduous and colossal Franco-Russian preparations for war" which were proof to him of the approach of a Balkan war "in which we shall all become involved." That is why the Kaiser wanted "clarity."

Fourthly and finally, nowhere in his note does the Kaiser make the "explicit" assumption that England had "vital interests" in Turkey which the Germans would fight over.

In short, Zechlin is anxious to neutralize the Kaiser's note by attributing only local meaning to it. But in restricting the application of this note to a "local" question, Zechlin loses sight of the real significance of the note. He fails to see that the Balkans were regarded as the powder keg of Europe. Furthermore, Zechlin tempers some of the Kaiser's key words. He changes "assiduous and colossal . . . preparations for war" to "military build-up." He changes the Balkan war "in which we shall all become involved" to the realization of German demands "even if this should require the use of military pressure *in the event of*" a Balkan war.

It will have become clear that I did not "distort the quotation by abbreviating it," nor did I place it "in the wrong factual and interpretative context." It is my critic who has turned words and sentences upside down, transformed statements into their opposites, and artificially separated a "factual context" from the political one. This should not surprise us, for Zechlin believes "we cannot understand German policy if we first set out to show that it was guided by conscious planning and if we then charge this planning with self-deception and hybris." [13] In contrast to Zechlin, I would insist that we cannot understand German policy if we first set out to show that it was characterized by a conscious lack of planning and if we then interpret this lack of planning as fate, ineptitude, bewilderment, hope, anguish, and response to outside pressures.

13. *Ibid.,* p. 81.

GERHARD RITTER:
The Historian's Concern for the Present

> Opinions that are most widely accepted and matters that everyone regards as settled often require the closest examination.
>
> *Georg Christian Lichtenberg*

The methods of presentation analyzed above could be demonstrated time and again in Zechlin's discussion of revolutionization or of policy regarding separate peace treaties. But now I would like to turn to Gerhard Ritter, who was hailed at the Historical Convention in Berlin as the "old master" of German historians, and examine a few characteristic features of his approach. It is difficult to do justice to Ritter's subtle line of reasoning on the "tragedy of statesmanship" as he presents it in volume III of *Staatskunst und Kriegshandwerk* (*The Sword and the Scepter*), because Ritter—in contrast to Zechlin—makes no effort at all to be objective. For Ritter, the historian is still the self-appointed and committed national censor. He writes with anger when he is forced to recognize how inept Bethmann Hollweg was to let Germany initiate the war. Bethmann Hollweg was inept because—unlike Ritter's "national hero," Bismarck—he was not able to induce Germany's enemies "to impale themselves, as it were, in blind rage on his sword." [1] Ritter's preconceptions in the evaluation of the outbreak of the war become even more obvious in his analysis of Bethmann Hollweg's war policy. In contrast to Zechlin, Ritter is more open in his concern for the German nation; and along with this concern he also demonstrates a constant personal involvement, a constant desire to understand and forgive every action of the Germans, who seem to him to need understanding and forgiveness. He tries to gloss over any conflict between the ideas of 1914 and our present standard of national behavior by referring to the historical context in which these ideas arose and by asking us to put ourselves in the position of the men who formed them. Every annexation is minimized or made to seem unimportant because it represents an "exception," not the rule. Consequently, its real significance is lost. When he cannot possibly conceal what he considers to be excessive German desires for power, he avoids the entire issue by invoking the Fates. The intent of his presentation is obvious. Ritter hopes to prevent the pendulum from swinging from the "exaggerated patriotism of former times" to what he calls "a critical attitude toward the German character and a portrayal of the German past [1914–18!] which shows that past in a negative light," a portrayal that Ritter thinks "could prove dangerous." [2] I take Ritter's comment as a slandering of German history rather than of me, because the period 1914–18, to which he refers here, by no means represents "the German past" as a whole. In the analysis of "his war" and "his chancellor," Ritter uses a number of methods to adapt grandiose imperialistic ideas to the vocabulary and thinking of 1964. These methods range from deliberate understatement of these ideas to tendentious alteration of meaning. For example, he claims that "the defensive character" of the September memorandum "is expressed in the very first sentence." This is true if

---

1. G. Ritter, *Der erste Weltkrieg*, p. 15.
2. *Ibid.*, p. 11.

"securing Germany's position in the east and the west for all time" is taken in its literal but not in its historical meaning. The "defensive character" of "security" in this case meant "that France be so weakened that she cannot revive as a great power" and that Russia "be pushed back as far as possible from the German border and her dominion over the non-Russian vassal nations broken."

I do not want to discuss this characteristic feature of Ritter's view of history any further. Instead, I shall turn to some basic methodological disagreements. At the Berlin historical convention, much was made of Ritter's methodological criticism, and my Waterloo was prophesied. Now that Ritter's book has been published, a critical and detailed debate is possible. We can begin with Ritter's analysis of Falkenhayn's attitudes in November 1915. Ritter claims that in a conversation with the Kaiser Falkenhayn designated as indispensable in future wars a line of deployment that would extend from Ostend to Metz and that the research of the General Staff had shown to be suitable, but that Falkenhayn "was not committed to this idea himself." [3] We do not need to refer to the sources to show how inconsistent Ritter's formulation is. If something is regarded as "essential," then an individual's "personal reservations" are immaterial to the facts of the case, however important they may be for a moral judgment of that individual. Ritter's presentation of Falkenhayn's attitude is misleading in other respects, too. Ritter makes it seem as if Falkenhayn was prepared to forego the line Ostend–Metz. But the documents reveal that Falkenhayn actually "needed" all of Belgium as a "glacis for a possible future war with the western powers." In the debate over the "nature" and "extent" of the "glacis," Falkenhayn was "personally for a strong occupation of Belgium." But Treutler, whose report we have, thought the Chief of the General Staff was "still willing to

---

3. G. Ritter, *Staatskunst und Kriegshandwerk,* vol. III, p. 606, note 2.

discuss the matter." [4] In short, my interpretation of the matter is the correct one.

Let us turn to another aspect of Ritter's historical method. In volume II, chapter X, of *Staatskunst und Kriegshandwerk,* Ritter examines the Austrian and German general staffs and their part in the outbreak of war in 1914. In this connection, he asserts, first, that "neither the Chief of the General Staff [Moltke] nor the minister of war [Falkenhayn] at any time wanted to bring about war," and, second, that German leaders, including Moltke, "showed little inclination to support a preventive war against Serbia" in 1913. The assassination at Sarajevo is the event that supposedly caused a sudden change in attitude. The Austro-Hungarian chief of staff, Conrad, receives all the blame for consistently urging a preventive strike.[5] A brief survey of the documents will test the validity of this thesis.

On December 23, 1908, Kaiser Franz Joseph gave Conrad permission to contact the German chief of staff in writing to prepare for the possibility "of military action in the Balkans, then against Russia and Italy." [6] Moltke answered Conrad that the main German offensive would be against France and observed that "the moment will soon come when the patience of the Habsburg monarchy toward Serbian provocations will end." Austria-Hungary would then have to march into Serbia, Russia would intervene, and the *"casus foederis* for Germany" would have occurred. "When Russia mobilizes," Moltke writes, "Germany will mobilize her entire army." Mobilization meant war for Germany, and in response, France would have to mobilize, too. But "two mobilized armies like those of Germany and France will not be able to exist side by side without

---

4. A. Scherer and J. Grunewald, *L'Allemagne et les problèmes de la paix pendant la première guerre mondiale,* vol. I (Paris, 1962), no. 159.

5. G. Ritter, *Staatskunst und Kriegshandwerk,* vol. II, pp. 282, 283, 290.

6. Conrad, *Aus meiner Dienstzeit,* vol. I, p. 631.

fighting." [7] The progression in this line of argument becomes evident in Moltke's memorandum of July 28, 1914,
to Bethmann Hollweg.[8] The key sentence reads: "If conflict
between Austria and Russia is inevitable, Germany will
mobilize and be prepared to go to war on two fronts." [9]
Thus, Moltke recognized the consequences of an Austro-
Hungarian invasion of Serbia and was ready to go a step
further; i.e., he was ready to back Austria-Hungary and to
respond to a partial Russian mobilization with a total German mobilization.

Both Conrad and Moltke had always favored a preventive strike against Serbia. After the Bosnian crisis of
1908–9 Moltke regretted "deeply . . . that an opportunity
had been missed that would not present itself again under
such a favorable aspect." Even if Russia "had taken action," Moltke reasoned, the "conditions" for war were "better now" than later. Moltke held firmly to this point of view
in the years that followed,[10] but he always insisted that "the
attack" would have to "come from the Slavs." [11] In the period from 1909 to 1913, he repeatedly stated his earlier
"belief that sooner or later a European war has to come in
which the ultimate issue will be a struggle between the Germanic and Slavic cultures." According to Moltke, and
Bethmann Hollweg as well, "to prepare for such a war is
the duty of all nations that are standard bearers of German
culture." [12] The only difference between Moltke and Bethmann Hollweg was that the latter assumed, in Kageneck's
words, "that after two or three years England would not
intervene." [13] Finally, in the spring of 1914, Conrad visited
Moltke; and Moltke told him, two months before the out-

7. *Ibid.*, p. 381.
8. I. Geiss, *Julikrise und Kriegsausbruch 1914,* vol. II, no. 659, pp. 262 ff.
9. *Ibid.*, p. 263.
10. Conrad, vol. I, p. 165.
11. Conrad, vol. III, p. 147.
12. *Ibid.*, pp. 146 f.
13. *Ibid.*, pp. 146 f., 151 f.

break of war, "that any delay meant a lessening of our prospects." [14] As far as Moltke was concerned, all diplomatic negotiations since 1909 had been "only a postponement but no solution." [15]

Even on the basis of this brief evidence, it is possible to draw certain conclusions:

1. It is incorrect to assert that the German General Staff never wanted to bring about a war. On the contrary, we know that from January 1909 on the staff clearly desired armed conflict despite the risk of world war it entailed. This desire remained until July 1914 when it became a reality.

2. It is inexact to write that in 1913 Germany "showed little inclination to support a preventive war against Serbia." One has to add "at this point" to indicate that only after England had been neutralized would Germany have considered the time ripe for a confrontation with Serbia and, consequently, for a European conflict. But Ritter never calls attention to this point.

3. It is wrong to assert that only Conrad welcomed war against Serbia and "disregarded the danger of a great conflagration." Moltke welcomed it, too, and he was equally unconcerned about the danger involved.

4. It is wrong to claim that Moltke's letter of January 1909, "despite appearances, did not really" issue a "carte blanche for any and every Balkan adventure." This tortuous formulation conceals the fact that the prospect of a future military action in the Balkans was held out to the Austrian politicians. This prospect was both consolation and encouragement for them.

5. It is misleading to emphasize Conrad's aggressive tendencies and to play down Moltke's.

The "deep shadows" of which Ritter speaks with emotion in the preface to volume II of *Staatskunst und Kriegs-*

14. *Ibid.*, p. 670.
15. *Ibid.*, p. 328.

handwerk (*The Sword and the Scepter*) are even deeper than he is able to recognize. His memories of former German glory are still so sacred to him that he wants to preserve them even at the price of tendentious distortion, often combining this loyalty to the past with vicious attacks on me. Ritter's interpretation of Zimmermann's memorandum of November 27, 1914, is a case in point.[16] Ritter criticizes my extensive résumé of this important memorandum and insinuates that I was "eager" to give it an "imperialistic" bias which, according to Ritter, it does not have. Consequently, I "failed to recognize" the true intent of the memorandum. Ritter claims, though he is careful not to elaborate on the point, that Zimmermann pursued moderate goals in this memo.

If we compare Ritter's paraphrase of this memorandum with the document itself, we find to our surprise that Ritter presents only *one* of Zimmermann's ideas, namely, that Zimmermann "flatly rejects the idea of a separate peace with Russia." Zimmermann first wanted to solidify "the existing front line" against France in the west and to force a decision in the east. Only then could a separate peace with Russia be considered. But Ritter does not say that Zimmermann wanted to carry on the war until both Russia and England were permanently weakened and could be contained. Zimmermann's memorandum reads: "Because our decision to fight to the death with England is firm and generally accepted, I see no need here for further discussion of the reasons behind it." Thus, what Ritter has not said is that Zimmermann wanted to defeat Russia first, or—if that could not be fully accomplished—that he wanted to impose a separate peace on Russia and go on to defeat England. Ritter also does not say that Zimmermann thought a separate peace with Russia could jeopardize German victory over England. There was a danger that Turkey (an ally "which

16. G. Ritter, *Staatskunst und Kriegshandwerk,* vol. III, pp. 62, 589, note 18.

could help us greatly against our enemies with its army of 800,000 men, its fleet, and its followers of Mohammed in the Near East and in Africa whom the declaration of a Holy War has roused to fanaticism") might regard such a peace as a betrayal and refuse further support for a German war against England. Nor does Ritter mention Zimmermann's stressing that Germany had "not only a political but also an important economic interest" in maintaining a friendship with Turkey. In Zimmermann's opinion, Germany had to make a point of "retaining and extending our area of commercial activity in Turkey," especially in view of difficulties anticipated in England and in the English colonies after the war.

Also, Ritter's introductory remarks on this document are misleading. He implies that Zimmermann's rejection of a separate peace with Russia was the result of "great skepticism" ("indeed more than skepticism") regarding the Tsar's disposition to make peace. This is a misleading interpretation of the facts. Zimmermann actually justified his rejection of a separate peace with Russia purely in terms of Germany's goals (security of Germany, of Austria-Hungary, and of Turkey), goals which would have been greatly endangered, or made unattainable, by the conclusion of peace with a Russia not decisively defeated. Finally, Ritter's concluding remarks on this document are incorrect. He implies that Zimmermann—in contrast to Falkenhayn, "who considered England and France our real and most dangerous opponents"—thought that, in the last analysis, Russia was the most dangerous enemy. But in fact, as Zimmermann made eminently clear, he "regarded England and Russia . . . (our two main enemies, next to France) . . . as equals."

Let me summarize: Ritter communicates to his reader neither the contents of the whole memorandum nor the substance of my paraphrase. Thus, the reader is in no position to make a critical comparison. This is a favorite device of Ritter's historiography, and he uses it here in an attempt to lend additional authority to his criticism. He goes so far as to claim that my "extensive résumé" changed the intent of the memorandum. Ritter either seeks to accuse me of falsification or postulates that I should have foregone complete summary of the document so that its "imperialistic bias" would not be revealed. But where Ritter is guided by the principle of duty and service to the fatherland, I choose to serve the higher principle of historical truth.

In Ritter's analysis of Solf's letters of August 28 and September 25, 1914—an analysis that serves as a criticism of my interpretation—we find the same method of omission and the same tailoring of documents to fit the historical picture of a moderate and tentative war aims policy. Ritter makes Solf appear to be a representative of the group which ridiculed "the annexationist hunger of otherwise moderate people" and rejected the "apostles of Germanization." [17] Solf did not think territorial gains in Europe useful since they might well complicate the acquisition of new colonies. Ritter accuses me of touching only indirectly on Solf's opposition to European annexations so that I could concentrate on his plans for colonial acquisitions and thus "give the impression of unrestrained imperialism."

What does the document actually say? Ritter does not deal with the real theme of Solf's letters, i.e., Solf's suggestions for "partitioning the African possessions of France, Belgium, and Portugal," nor does he discuss these suggestions in the context in which they belong. Two pages later he writes: "Solf . . . was interested in large territorial acquisitions only overseas." Ritter also distorts the context of

17. *Ibid.*, p. 593, note 35. Vietsch, too, has recently portrayed Solf as a kind of ideal German of moderate leanings because, in the course of the war, Solf, like Hans Delbrück, came to reject the rabid enmity toward England that characterized the navy, the fanatical adherents of U-boat warfare, and the representatives of the warship industry.

Solf's suggestions "for the improvement of Germany's western borders. These suggestions took the form of a map and projected limited German acquisitions." We can see already how much Ritter has changed the context to minimize the importance of Solf's letters. Ritter does not mention that Jagow had solicited Solf's suggestions, nor does he take into account that, as minister for colonial affairs, Solf was responsible for matters of colonial acquisition and that his suggestions must be seen in this light. Ritter presents Solf's statements as merely personal opinion and ignores the circumstances under which the letters were written. They must be seen in connection with the September program for which Solf acted as "the expert" on a "consolidated colonial empire in central Africa." Ritter censures me for making only "passing reference" to Solf's opposition to continental annexations. He puts unwarranted stress on this opposition to throw Solf's "conciliatory" spirit into exaggerated relief and to convince the reader that Solf, because of his opposition to "the apostles of Germanization," was the very soul of conciliation and moderation. Ritter can do this only by disregarding the interdependence of official roles, personal opinions, and the facts of the situation. But a unified grasp of all these factors is essential to our understanding, particularly in Solf's case. If the unified picture I try to present in *Griff nach der Weltmacht* creates the "impression of unrestrained imperialism" for Ritter or —as he fears—for other readers of my book, I would suggest that such an impression can arise only if the reader assumes the role of censor rather than scholar.

I am grateful to Professor Ritter for pointing out to me an incorrect emphasis in my interpretation of Loebell's memorandum of October 29, 1914 (see Ritter's paper given in Berlin in October 1964 and *Staatskunst und Kriegshandwerk*, III, 593, n. 38). Ritter correctly objects to my statement that at this time Loebell "emphatically advocated extensive annexations in the east, particularly in the Baltic provinces and in Lithuania" (*Griff nach der Weltmacht,* 3rd ed., p. 133). I regret that, influenced by Loebell's later advocacy of a Polish border strip policy, I overemphasized the rudiments of this policy in his memorandum of October 1914. But I regret even more that my error prompted Ritter to characterize Loebell "as a basically anti-annexationist minister" (*Staatskunst*, III, 45). Nothing could be further from the truth. The memorandum of October 1914, which Ritter himself quotes at length, shows Loebell to be an advocate of ambitious programs in Africa (i.e., in the French and Belgian Congo). It also demonstrates that Loebell was eager to win permanent control over a defeated France by French cession of the territory east of the Maas (Liège and environs) to Prussia. He also wanted to assure some form of control over Belgium to "give Germany free access to France if at all possible." He was willing to give up this plan only if Belgium proved to be the crucial bargaining point for winning an "acceptable" peace from a tenacious England, a peace that would guarantee "the freedom of the seas" and German overseas interests. He was able to say of France:

France has been Germany's enemy throughout history. . . . If this is to change in the future, we must weaken the human potential and the territorial and economic power of France so thoroughly and permanently that she will have neither the means nor strength to engage again in conspiracies leading to military actions against us. Peace in the west is a matter of life and death for us, and we must secure this peace primarily at the expense of France. This decision is facilitated by the fact that France has the most to offer us.[18]

Loebell, an "extreme conservative," shared Tirpitz's view that England, not Russia, was Germany's main enemy. It seemed "ultimately desirable" to him "for England, like

18. E. Volkmann, *Die Annexionsfragen des Weltkrieges, Werk des Untersuchungsausschusses*, ser. 4, vol. 12 / 1 (Berlin, 1929). Loebell's memorandum of October 29, 1914, appears on pp. 187 ff. The passage quoted is from p. 188.

Japan, to remain exposed to sustained pressure which can be exerted only by a cooperative Russia." Loebell thought Russia had to remain "a significant factor in power politics" so that we (Germany) "can make her serve our global political interests." This extremely conservative Prussian's desire to use Russia as a pawn in Germany's political game did not, however, deter him after mid-1915 from emphatically demanding a border strip whose Germanization he wanted to initiate administratively during the war. This plan was anticipated in the memorandum of October 1914 when Loebell demanded "better protection of the East Prussian border on the Niemen and Narew" [19] and still later when he demanded the strictest dependence of the newly founded Kingdom of Poland on Germany.[20]

This concludes my discussion of methodological questions. It has become clear that what Zechlin and Ritter sanctify as a historically critical and objective method is in fact method with a motive. In summary, I would like to make the following observations. In view of the overwhelming unanimity of the evidence demonstrating the German nation's desire for power and its sense of mission, Ritter's and Zechlin's concern for the moral crises and fatalistic sighs of a Bethmann Hollweg or a Kühlmann seems to me a one-sided approach. I would suggest, too, that the historian should avoid emotional and moralizing adjectives such as "painful, upsetting, shocking, rash, deluded, disastrous, fateful." He should also avoid concepts like "fate, destiny, doom, and tragedy," which fade into the incomprehensible and metaphysical, for it is the historian's particular task to clarify—as far as human understanding and the resources of scholarship can—the complex course of historical events in which the individual is only one factor and certainly not the only decisive one.

19. *Ibid.*, pp. 191 f.
20. F. Fischer, *Griff nach der Weltmacht*, pp. 594 f.

Index